Presented To:

_____

From:

_____

Date:

_____

GOD'S

PLAN FOR OUR SUCCESS NEHEMIAH'S

WAY

GOD'S

PLAN FOR OUR SUCCESS NEHEMIAH'S

WAY

Rebuilding

the Gates

in Your

Christian Journey

CONNIE HUNTER-URBAN

DESTINY IMAGE® PUBLISHERS, INC.

P.O. Box 310, Shippensburg, PA 17257-0310

"Promoting Inspired Lives."

This book and all other Destiny Image, Revival Press, MercyPlace, Fresh Bread, Destiny Image Fiction, and Treasure House books are available at Christian bookstores and distributors worldwide.

For a U.S. bookstore nearest you, call 1-800-722-6774.

For more information on foreign distributors, call 717-532-3040.

Reach us on the Internet: www.destinyimage.com.

ISBN 13 TP: 978-0-7684-4108-6

ISBN 13 Ebook: 978-0-7684-8858-6

For Worldwide Distribution, Printed in the U.S.A.

1 2 3 4 5 6 7 8 / 16 15 14 13 12

ACKNOWLEDGMENTS

I would like to thank the following people for their support:

The Lord, with whom I am in love.

My wonderful husband, Wade, who is always ready with Scripture, words of encouragement, and help in general.

My daughters, Jillian and Jennifer, who have provided me with more richness than I could ever imagine.

My Bible study group, who were the first to learn about the gates as God was putting this study on my heart.

The Tuesday night intercessory group, who prayed a contract into existence.

My friends, Margie and Curtis, who both went through the gates journey with me.

And my sister, Lynda, who has mentored me through many things.

I would especially like to thank my mother, who was my inspiration for being a godly woman. She started me out and was with me for each step of my own gates journey. In the weeks before she passed away, I sat at her bedside, revised the manuscript, and read aloud. She was my encourager, even until the end.

ENDORSEMENTS

I met Connie about 15 years ago at a women's conference in Bath, Indiana. She is very dedicated to the Body of Christ. She has given her heart to the Kingdom of God, working diligently to help men, women, and families be all that Christ has ordained them to be. She moves in the gifts of the Spirit as the Holy Spirit moves upon her. She is a dedicated warrior in the Kingdom of God, and I know she is a powerful tool in the hand of the Lord against all the wicked devices of the enemy. She continues to work hard, hosting services and conferences, and teaching women. I know that Connie is sold out to Christ and His work, and to help others. I pray that He continues to bless her and establish her in all she sets forth to do.

Sister Vonda Bishop
Evangelist and Speaker

I have known Connie Hunter-Urban for many years now as my friend, mentor, and teacher. This teaching on "The Gates" started an awakening in my heart and caused me to hunger for a deeper walk with the Lord. For me and others, it began a new quest for the glory of God to manifest in our lives. And it most definitely did!

Jo Ellen Stevens
Retreat Speaker and Home Church Pastor
Connersville, Indiana

Connie Hunter-Urban has been one of the most inspirational women of God whom I have ever had the privilege of knowing. She and I have been friends since childhood when our families attended church together. She has been a constant woman of faith and has grown into an incredible teacher of God's Word.

Connie recently taught "The Gates" workshop at the church we pastor, Positive Impact Worldwide in Saint Petersburg, Florida. Her tremendous skill in communicating the Word of God and its meaning was comparable to the best of Bible scholars. It kept the students on the edge of their seats thirsting for more of God's wisdom. Our congregation has requested us to please book Connie again! It will be our pleasure to have Connie back to bring a fresh revelation of God's Word.

Pastors Jay and Kara'lynne Brubaker
Positive Impact Worldwide Church
St. Petersburg, Florida

Every once in a while we may be blessed to meet a true member of God's "Special Team," one of those very rare, spiritually in tune, uniquely gifted, and precisely handcrafted vessels of honor, whose teaching and anointing—through love and passion, godly character, sensitivity, submission, and uncompromising personal integrity—makes a truly profound impact upon our life. Individuals who are specifically entrusted by Father to administer the "secret things of the Most High" are few and far between. These "secret things" are rare finds, not easily discerned and received by all. Vessels with this extraordinary calling are interested only in pleasing the Father, in bringing honor and glory to His name. They genuinely, with their own lives as living testimonies, fulfill this calling in accordance with the very purpose and heartbeat of God. This describes well the life, teaching, and ministry of my friend, Connie Hunter-Urban. I could not support, endorse, or recommend her intrinsic, God-gifted personal qualifications highly enough!

Karl Tobien
Author, *Dancing Under the Red Star*

Contents

Foreword 13

Prologue 15

Introduction 19

CHAPTER 1
The Sheep Gate: Falling in Love 23

CHAPTER 2
The Fish Gate: Sharing the News 39

CHAPTER 3
The Old Gate: Going Deeper 55

CHAPTER 4
The Valley Gate: Enduring the Trials 71

CHAPTER 5
The Dung (Refuse) Gate:
Refining Our Character 87

CHAPTER 6
The Fountain Gate: Getting Filled 99

CHAPTER 7
The Water Gate: Devouring the Word 117

CHAPTER 8
The Horse Gate: Doing Warfare 135

CHAPTER 9
The East Gate: Fostering Worship 149

CHAPTER 10
The Gate of Miphkad:
Fulfilling Our Destiny. 165

EPILOGUE
by Wade Urban 181

APPENDIX 1
Map of Jerusalem 183

APPENDIX 2
Levels of Ezekiel's River 187

APPENDIX 3
The Wilderness Tabernacle Chart 191

APPENDIX 4
The Wilderness Tabernacle. 195

Endnotes. 199

FOREWORD

"Roll over at 3 months, sit up at 6 months, crawl by 9 months, and walk by 12 months." These are the words my mother used to describe a baby's growth. Though it varied from child to child, I appreciated the general rule of thumb that helped me understand if my baby's development was roughly on target, on her way to becoming a mature adult.

That's what Connie's book does, too. It helps us understand our spiritual growth: *that* we should grow, *how* we should grow, and what's happening at each stage *while* we grow. And it is Nehemiah's system of measurement that Connie uses to provide the framework. It's as if Nehemiah tacked a growth chart to the wall to represent the spiritual developmental process:

1. Falling in love with Jesus

2. Sharing the Good News

3. Digging deeper

4. Enduring the trials

5. Refining our character

6. Getting filled

7. Devouring the Word

8. Doing warfare

9. Fostering worship

10. Fulfilling our destiny

How reassuring it is to look at the timeless pages of Scripture and recognize that God had us in mind when He inspired Nehemiah to pen his words. Connie uses real-life stories and humor, together with Bible truths, to make these essential steps applicable, doable, measurable, and personally achievable.

In the process, readers get to see how each segment becomes part of the whole journey to be like Christ and to accomplish the work they were created to do. Everything this book teaches propels readers toward their individual, specific purpose. As Howard G. Hendricks once said, "[God] wants to minister *through* you. But before [He] can ever minister through you, [He] must minister *to* you."

Showing us how to allow God to minister *to* us is what Connie accomplishes so masterfully. It's an old message told in a new, fresh, and individual way. I see the reading of this book as a turning point for countless men and women in their walks of faith with Christ.

Lynda Hunter-Bjorklund

PROLOGUE

Being a Christian is the part of me with which I most identify. Throughout my life, even when I was not close to God, He was always my friend and confidant. Sometimes, however, I haven't seen the growth I felt I needed in Him. Whenever I became discouraged, I comforted myself with the story of building our house. Many years ago, my husband and I contracted for a new home to replace the home we had lost in a fire at Christmastime. We spent hours planning the house and going all over our area to check for just the right cabinets, siding, flooring, and lighting. As the harsh winter lingered on that year, I waited impatiently to get going on our new family abode.

Finally, spring arrived, and the hard terrain had thawed enough to allow workers to break ground. I began counting days until my husband, children, and I could move from the trailer where we were living in town into our emerging masterpiece out in the country. A foundation was dug; footers were poured. Each day as I saw the house taking shape, my impatience grew.

I was at the site for one of my multiple visits each day when the men framed the walls. Suddenly, it looked like a house, and I was ecstatic. "It's not going to be long now," I announced to the contractor, rubbing my hands and smiling excitedly.

He just looked at me. I'm sure he was frustrated by my growing enthusiasm to get into our evolving home in the country. He just shook his head. "It's still gonna be quite a while," he said. "Now comes the part where ya can't see anything happenin'." He proceeded to tell me about the wiring, plumbing, and roofing. My heart dropped.

Days turned into weeks, then months. Despite my anxiousness, though, I realized if they didn't do those foundational things, our house wouldn't be solid in the end. I could choose the perfect wallpaper and coordinating window treatments, but that would mean nothing without the basics to make our house strong. When they finished months later, we not only had a place that looked good but was also well-built and sturdy.

It's the same with our Christian house. At times we seem to be growing in leaps and bounds, but then come those times when we can't see anything God is doing in us. He is, however, at work. There may be stretches when He's creating patience, fortitude, or one of many things that will sustain us in our walk with Him. Building us into the person He wants us to be takes time and is a series of slow but essential steps. Just because we can't see anything happening doesn't mean that what He's building at those times is any less valuable than His more visible work. It all goes together to shape us into His beautifully crafted creation.

Two summers ago my husband and I were visiting a church in Richmond, Indiana, where the pastor talked about the wall being rebuilt in the Book of Nehemiah. I have loved and taught that book for many years, for its depths provide a number of principles for successful Kingdom living. When I got home and reread the Scriptures the pastor had discussed about repairing the wall of our city, the Lord spoke into my spirit and said, "What about the gates?" Over the next few weeks, the ten references to the gates in Nehemiah 3 thrilled me as I researched more and more information. What is laid out in these gates is the progression of our walk in Christ. Just like my experience with building our house, it's an analogy for our growth as Christians. Even those times when we don't see the building going on inside us are part of the growth process that ultimately brings us into our destiny in God.

Desiring to grow in God is a decision we all must make for ourselves. Once we do, we discover our walk with Him is not a sprint but a marathon. To grow deeper in Him is a bits-and-pieces process. Rushing that progression means we choose to settle for a false finish line, which could later stunt our growth. As Nehemiah rebuilds the wall, he exemplifies the one-brick-at-a-time approach to our journey. He lays out benchmarks for our success if we proceed steadily as God has prescribed. I've been a Christian my entire life, and this study changed my life as I've seen what God so clearly delineated for my Christian growth.

In my own Christian walk, I've observed new and old believers with varying degrees of commitment to God. Often, especially baby Christians get the steps of this journey with God out of order, become discouraged, and then give up. Just as a baby becomes a toddler, a child, a teen, and an adult, so does a Christian go through growing steps. We wouldn't expect an infant to eat a steak or run a race, but often the Church expects baby Christians to be immediately mature. By the same token, if a baby *never* grew up or continued to eat formula when he was a teen or adult, development would be unnatural. Many 50-year-old Christians, however, are still not eating the meat of God's Word or growing deeper in Him.

As I began a study on the first gate, God's truth started to speak to me and continued throughout each of the gates. After I finished, my husband and I began a home Bible study on the gates. As God's message unfolded, people understood how their walk with God fit the progression of the gates. The reaction was amazing. People often referred to their current experiences in terms of the gate they were occupying—the Valley Gate, the Dung Gate, or others. Each week, God gave more revelation to us—all the way through the final gate. People knew God had anointed this study and that it had spoken to them at whatever point they currently were residing.

Definitions provided are from Strong's Concordance. The *Dugan King James Version* supplied most meanings of names of the repairers of the gates who give clues to facets of our walk.

I hope God lavishly blesses you through what He has revealed to me. As I teach you about growing in Him through the framework of the gates, may He speak to you about your own walk, reinforcing strong areas while showing you which gates may require more attention so your journey toward your destiny won't be later impeded.

INTRODUCTION

A lot of times, I've wished life came with a road map—how to be a good neighbor, employee, parent, wife/husband. For most of our lives, we're on our own for how to maximize what we want to accomplish. God's Word isn't like that, though. It is filled with clues and blueprints for how to make our lives richer while growing into His purpose for us.

The lives of men like David and Joseph show how God places a call which He eventually brings into fruition. However, although God had a plan for both these men, years passed before they saw those calls fulfilled. During those times, they went through many experiences that probably made them wonder if God was still watching out for them and bringing them to their promised destinies. Though the outcome seemed uncertain at times, a greater purpose was unfolding. God was creating growth to allow them to be rulers who would lead His people. Their characters were being built during the journey they had with God.

Nehemiah 3 is one representation of a blueprint for our walk in God's Kingdom. Around 445 B.C., Nehemiah, which means "repentance of the Lord," was the cupbearer for the Persian king, Artaxerxes (see Neh. 2:1).[1] When he became aware of how the walls had fallen into disrepair around Jerusalem, the city in which he was born, he began to grieve. God then put it in his heart to rebuild them. He went to Artaxerxes to tell of his desire to spearhead the walls' repair (even though he risked execution by showing emotion before the king as his cupbearer). Not only was he not killed, he found favor to receive time off, letters for lumber, an armed guard, and access to regions he needed to pass through on his way.

Nehemiah began the project as all of us should when we receive a call from God. He didn't share his vision until he was ready to begin the work (see Neh. 2:12). Sometimes when God gives us a vision of His plan for us, keeping that vision to ourselves can spare us sorrow. People who don't possess a similar vision often say discouraging things and can dissuade us from our assignment in God. We should also recognize the power of words in accomplishing or derailing God's purpose. Once Nehemiah did tell others, he was opposed by people (Sanballat and Tobiah) who ridiculed, undermined, and fought God's work. As he began his duty, he proceeded in the confidence of God—and, with other Jewish families, repaired the wall and ten gates in Jerusalem in 52 days. Clearly, being in God's will and acting in one accord with others can accomplish much.

Cities were often located on a hill, and their walls were their most outstanding component.[2] They were so strong that today they're often what archaeologists discover in ruins. For instance, they have found remnants of Nehemiah's wall that were many feet thick at places. In Bible times, walls showed a city's prosperity and God's sanction or His curse; a broken wall signified God had negatively judged that city.[3] Gates, however, were the weakest point of the wall, so that's where enemies usually attacked. Around our own Christian walls, the gates we enter are a place of vulnerability to the enemy, too. When we decide to go through another gate to a new level in Him, we can expect a battle to ensue. I've often heard that with new levels come new devils.

Ancient gates were made of wood (which represents human effort) and bronze (which represents strength because it's hard for making utensils and resists fire). Bronze probably made the gates less vulnerable to attack from fire.[4] They were bound with plates of copper (which represents softness and pliability). All these substances possess traits that describe us, too. We're human; we possess strength in Christ to go through the fire; yet we must be pliable enough to be changed.

Allowing God to remake us is the greatest part of growing in Him. We can't stay the same and mature simultaneously.

The gates in Jerusalem served many purposes:[5]

- Markets were there (sheep, fish).

- Visitors were received / rejected.

- People in positions of authority sat there.

- People met for social / legal / public events.

- Judgment occurred there.

- Legal events happened there, such as when Boaz bargained for Ruth with his near kinsman (see Ruth 4:1-12).

- It was a gathering place. Proverbs 31:31 discusses this in its praise of the virtuous woman at the city gates.

Jesus referred to gates when He said to stay holy and...

Enter ye in at the strait gate: for wide is the gate, and broad is the way, that leadeth to destruction, and many there be which go in thereat: because strait is the gate, and narrow is the way, which leadeth unto life, and few there be that find it (Matthew 7:13-14).

By coming into this Christian journey, we're choosing a road that's straight and narrow. His use of the gates to show the difference between a Christian's and sinner's choices emphasizes that He expects us to maintain a separated lifestyle, and the gates allow us to stay focused on Him and the righteous life He requires. Our problems seem unique to us at times, but other Christians must also travel along the same growth path as we. David said,

Open to me the gates of righteousness: I will go into them, and I will praise the Lord: this gate of the Lord, into which the righteous shall enter (Psalm 118:19-20).

In essence, gates are crucial for us to walk through, and if we understand how they progress, our walk is bound to be more successful.

Gates have many purposes, both symbolically and practically. If Jerusalem represents the Church–and we are the Church—then the wall represents our walk with God. Just like Nehemiah's walls, at times the wall around our own city, or spiritual man, is in need of repair, so God sends someone or something to accomplish that task. Within that wall are many places where we graduate into the next phase of our time with God. Those are our gates. Though other gates are mentioned in Scripture, Nehemiah 3 lists ten from which we can glean instruction. Each gate in Nehemiah's wall has a specific meaning that parallels phases of our Christian walk. We come through the first gate as new Christians and go through each of the other gates on our way toward the last one—our assignment in Him.

When we rear our children, we're bringing them into their own place as adults. Therefore, we must consider where we want them to end up before they get there. We give them the right foods, spiritual direction, work ethic, study skills, education. We teach solid character traits: honesty, responsibility, integrity. We encourage and discipline until they've grown and can use all they have learned. This doesn't happen one day when we awaken and say, "Hmm, I think I want my children to be good adults." It's a years-long process. The same goes with God. Too many think that one day we become born again, and then God turns us loose to somehow evolve into mature Christians. On the contrary, He has a plan for our success, and the gates delineate that, step by step, experience by experience, brick by brick. The gates' progression is important when we're just beginning and want to have benchmarks for how to proceed, when we're strong but want to grow stronger, or when our city lies in *"waste, and the gates thereof are burned with fire"* (Neh. 2:17). We need a plan to allow us to grow in Him. This book gives Nehemiah's blueprint.

CHAPTER

1

THE SHEEP GATE: FALLING IN LOVE

Then Eliashib the high priest rose up with his brethren the priests, and they builded the sheep gate; they sanctified it, and set up the doors of it; even unto the tower of Meah they sanctified it, unto the tower of Hananeel (Nehemiah 3:1).

And between the going up of the corner unto the sheep gate repaired the goldsmiths and the merchants (Nehemiah 3:32).

My parents came to the Lord before I was born, so I can't remember a time when we didn't go to church frequently or have the Lord as the center of our lives. I do, however, recall when I surrendered my life to Him as an adult. Just out of college, I spent a year trying to make up for all the fun experiences I felt my Christian upbringing had caused me to miss. But every relationship, activity, and pursuit led me nowhere but back to my need for God. During this time I realized for myself that I wanted God to be the center of my life. Many people flirt around with Him before they realize that selling out to God is the answer to the void inside. Something happens when we finally understand that Christ gave His life for us: we want to give ours to Him. We become a new creation.

At the time, I hadn't been working long at my teaching job in Connersville, Indiana. My driving partner and I were always trying to find shorter routes for our 30-minute commute. Finally, we discovered a curvy, little-driven country road that shaved off a few minutes. We became quite adept at maneuvering through twists among cornfields as we drove the route every afternoon for two months. One morning I went in to work by myself and decided to try the road going to and not just from my job. I'd traversed the same route every afternoon for eight weeks; but because I was going the opposite direction, it seemed like a new one.

So it is with giving our lives to God. When we're born again, we turn around and go a different direction though we're still in the same territory. We live in the same house, work at the same job, shop at the same stores; but now everything is different and new. We have new perspectives, desires, and hopes. We see the world through Christ's eyes and can never go back to the barrenness of what we once desired.

THE SHEEP GATE

In Nehemiah 3, the first gate of the wall that was repaired was the Sheep Gate. The foundation for all other gates we go through is salvation, for the gate of salvation, Jesus, is where we all begin our Kingdom trek. As a matter of fact, He said, *"...He that entereth not by the door into the sheepfold, but climbeth up some other way, the same is a thief and a robber"* (John 10:1). All of us must be born again one way—through Jesus Christ (see John 14:6). His death gave access to this entry point of our Christian journey. When we commit to making Jesus our Lord, He becomes our shepherd, and we become His sheep. The Sheep Gate was the first to be repaired, but it's also the only gate Nehemiah mentioned two times in this chapter. This repetition brings us full circle around the walls because everything starts and ends with Jesus. No matter where our journey takes us, we're never far from the Sheep Gate.

If you'll look at Appendix 1, the Sheep Gate was at the northwest corner near the temple and was rebuilt by *Eliashib,* which means "the God of conversion."[1] It had no locks, for this gate of salvation stays perpetually open for sinners to come in. One tower was placed on each side: *Meah,* also called the Tower of the Hundred, and *Hananeel,* "grace, or gift, of God."[2] Old Testament towers were an important part of a wall's defense. Each tower that was on the wall, including Meah and Hananeel, had a watchman, who provided protection against potential enemies or imminent problems. For me, the towers represent the diligence of those watchers (today we would call them intercessors); we probably came through the Sheep Gate by our intercessors' efforts. In essence, *Hananeel* or God's grace is at the gate as a convert enters. For many of us, Grandma or Mom and Dad were our watchers on the wall for us to come in this gate. We entered here as a result of God's grace and their watching over us and praying tirelessly for our salvation.

SACRIFICE

The Sheep Gate is synonymous with sacrifice. Since people brought sheep for sacrificing in through this gate, it was set aside as sacred. We, too, must become consecrated for God at this Sheep Gate. As we commit to our Shepherd, sacrifice is crucial, and that's a decision many struggle with. A lot of unsaved people wonder how they can possibly forfeit all they've ever known for Christ. That's a natural reaction because a lot of us are keepers—of old shoes, outdated clothes, useless "treasures." Now we choose to replace our desires and character with His, and we gain far more than we lose. Just as Jesus gave Himself, we start to change into what He wants us to become. When we truly repent, we don't long, like Lot's wife, for what was left behind. Our desires and goals simply become different. I've seen many people whose countenance has even changed. We give up the carnal side of ourselves to be transformed into whatever He wants us to become.

Jesus is our model of sacrifice. He *"was oppressed, and He was afflicted...He* [was] *brought as a lamb to the slaughter, and as a sheep before her shearers is dumb, so He* [opened] *not His mouth"* (Isa. 53:7; see also Acts 8:32). In Bible days, sacrificial lambs were spread out to be sacrificed in a cross position with their heads down. Hebrews were so accustomed to this sacrifice ritual that when John recited the words over Jesus—*"Behold the Lamb of God, which taketh away the sin of the world"* (John 1:29b)—they made a connection. As John baptized Jesus in Jordan and declared who He was, people had clues to Jesus' majesty; He was validated as Messiah for the first, but not the last time. He was the Lamb of God, our lamb who was also sacrificed on a cross. With Jesus as our model, when we surrender ourselves, we no longer retain the same interests, attitudes, or character—we give those up to take on Jesus' character. Romans 12:1 says to *"present your bodies a living sacrifice, holy, acceptable unto God."* Like Jesus, we must sacrifice ourselves for the new creature we become.

SHEEP'S SIGNIFICANCE

The first biblical reference to sheep (or livestock of any kind) is found in Genesis 4:2-4 when, Abel, their keeper, pleased God. I grew up in the Midwest, so I understand the value of livestock. Not having grown up on a farm, however, I'm limited in my appreciation of sheep. Despite what a farmer sees in them, I consider them less valuable than other animals. To me, they're dirty, dumb, and ugly. Perhaps God chose sheep to be a comparison to us because that's how we might be described before we accepted Jesus into lives. The world sees the negative in us, but not God. He doesn't look at us with the eye of the critical city slicker, but with the love of a Shepherd who adores His sheep. We should learn what God has to say about sheep since the Bible refers to them about 400 times—the most frequently mentioned animal in the Bible.[3] When Scripture deals so often with a topic, it usually holds a special meaning.

Sheep possess many traits similar to ours. First, they're raised in all places of the world, even dry places, because their bodies can adapt. I often hear Christians complain because they're not in the church, marriage, job, or city they'd really like to be in. That happens to all of us at different stages in our life's journey. We're sometimes in fertile places and sometimes in dry places, but we must learn to grow wherever we find ourselves. "Grow where you are planted" is good advice. Christian sheep exist throughout the nations; and even though some are still persecuted as much as the first century church was, those churches are thriving.

Second, sheep are neither intelligent nor wise. They get easily flustered and confused; sometimes, even when their flock is nearby, they can't make their way back to the others. In the world's estimation, that lack of intelligence is a negative trait, but God doesn't choose His sheep because they're the smartest or strongest He can find. As a matter of fact, it's just the opposite. Deuteronomy 7:7 says, *"The Lord did not set His love upon you, nor choose you, because ye were more in number than any people; for ye were the fewest of all people."* In other words, we're not the strongest He could find, but the most in need of help. Aimee Semple McPherson had emotional problems; William Branham was poor and "semiliterate"; and A.A. Allen had drinking issues.[4] The sheep He chooses and leads into a godly destiny are chosen in spite of and because of their weaknesses.

My husband and I once had a woman pastor to whom the Lord spoke frequently. He would sometimes reveal words to her that she didn't know the meanings or pronunciations of, so He'd spell them for her. God was obviously giving her revelation beyond her intellect so He could receive the praise. Despite their shortcomings, great men and women of God have been used mightily for His work. He picks us even though we're least because we're *teachable,* and His ability can shine through us. He wants us *because* we're weak and need the Shepherd to guide us. One great paradox of our Christianity is that *"God hath chosen the foolish things of the world to confound the wise"* (1 Cor. 1:27a). Sheep certainly fall into that group.

Sheep were also important to Hebrews for many other reasons. They provided food, cosmetics, clothes, wool, meat, leather, glue, soap, tallow, suet (fat for cooking), fertilizer, and catgut.[5] As sheep, we, too, can be used for many purposes even though we feel we have nothing to offer the Kingdom. We can be teachers, pastors, apostles, prophets, evangelists, intercessors, mentors, and a myriad of other things. Sometimes our job is just to clean the church, drive the bus to pick up children, or gather trash in the parking lot; nevertheless, *"whatsoever thy hand findeth to do, do it with thy might"* (Eccles. 9:10a). That's a lesson that will help us in all the gates—for each task we do for God, whether big or small, fosters characteristics God will ultimately use.

THE FLOCK

Sheep don't function well by themselves; they are made to be watched and cared for by the shepherd as part of his flock. They aren't creatures equipped to survive by themselves. As Christian sheep, we must find the support of a flock, or church. Paul cautioned us about *"forsaking the assembling of ourselves together"* because he realized we need fellowship as a crucial part of our maturing (Heb. 10:25). When my husband and I mentor young Christians, we stress the importance of being associated with a church flock. Many troubles new Christians encounter come because they didn't create a bond with other members of an assembly to whom they were accountable. If we foster a support system with the church flock, we can more successfully withstand problems that come along.

That doesn't mean our flock itself is without issues. In every group of animals (or even people) there's a pecking order to see who's fittest. For sheep, it's a butting order. The more domineering sheep vie for a higher place and butt away the lambs. Often, within both a sheep and church flock, more aggressive ones *"thrust with side and with shoulder, and* [push] *all the diseased with* [their] *horns, till* [they scatter] *them abroad"* (Ezek. 34:21). Overbearing sheep bully weaker ones, push them away from food or water, show jealousy, and do other aggressive acts like spoiling the pastures and water (see Ezek. 34:18).[6]

Sadly, all flocks have problems, but we still shouldn't go it alone. In every flock there's hope; when the shepherd shows up, things change because his presence brings peace to his sheep. As our Shepherd hovers over us, He's doing a work not only in us but also in those who cause contention, bullies high up in the butting order, to bring us all into His ways.

THE SHEPHERD

We used to sing a song called, "Kind Shepherd Lead Me." That title summarizes the relationship of sheep to Shepherd. He is kind and leads. Psalm 23 gives His definitive job description. He is the sheep's provision, and they *"shall not want"* (Ps. 23:1). He gives them rest and refreshment as they *"lie down in green pastures...beside the still waters"* (Ps. 23:2). He *"restoreth* [their] *soul"* and directs them on *"paths of righteousness"* (Ps. 23:3) that bring them into right relationship with Him. He comforts them with His presence even when death could be imminent so they experience *"no evil"* (Ps. 23:4). He ensures victory and feasting even *"in the presence of* [their] *enemies"* and ensures anointing and abundance as their *"cup runneth over"* (Ps. 23:5). He's the consummate leader for His sheep, and as a result, *"goodness and mercy shall follow* [them] *all the days"* of their lives (Ps. 23:6).

Here, at the Sheep Gate as we learn *about* our Shepherd, we learn total dependence *on* Him, a lesson that serves us through other gates, too. The Hebrew word for shepherd is *raah,* meaning "to tend a flock; ...to associate with (as a friend); ...companion, keep company with, ... make friendship with."[7] A shepherd is all these things for the sheep: overseer, leader, protector, friend, guide, authority figure, provider, and ever-present companion.[8] In essence, he is everything to them. Because he's all these roles for his flock, the shepherd and sheep grow such a bond that they know one another intimately. If sheep wander off or mix with another flock, the shepherd can call, and they *"hear his voice...and* [he] *leadeth them out...he goeth before them, and the sheep follow him: for they know his voice"* (John 10:3-4). Do we sometimes wander and mix with a flock we don't belong to? When we do, our Shepherd gently calls to us, and we can return. Here at the Sheep Gate we've become accustomed to the voice of our Shepherd, too.

Sheep depend entirely on the shepherd—for food, protection, water, shelter, and care.[9] We, too, must learn reliance on the Shepherd and understand that *"when* [we are] *weak, then* [we are] *strong"* (2 Cor. 12:10). Strength comes from knowing the Shepherd as the sum total of our lives. As Christians we find many opportunities to follow someone or something other than our Master, but the more we're with Him, the more we want to be there and nowhere else. When we spend time with our Shepherd, we learn not only His voice but also His practices and heart.

The Shepherd has a heart of love for His sheep. Sometimes He gently carries and nurtures those with special needs. He will *"gather the lambs with His arm, and carry them in His bosom, and shall gently lead those that are with young"* (Isa. 40:11). That describes all of us at times. Often when we feel strong and invulnerable, a crisis comes along that lets us know we need to run back to and rely on the Shepherd. At those times we're too weak to walk on our own, so He gathers us into His arms and carries us until we're strong again. At other times, we become pregnant with His design for us, and He must lead us through every step so His plans won't be aborted. In other threatening situations we also must rely on the Shepherd. Even within church settings, we're at the mercy of bears, wolves, and lions, but the Shepherd will protect us. He may *"send [us] forth as sheep in the midst of wolves"* (Matt. 10:16), but He's right there with us. Wisdom comes as we realize we must rely on Him to protect us. In His consummate care, He *"will seek that which was lost, and bring again that which was driven away, and will bind up that which was broken, and will strengthen that which was sick..."* (Ezek. 34:16). Our Shepherd is there for whatever weakness we possess, and He knows just how to reach us.

Several years ago, my sister who lives in Arizona met a man she ultimately fell in love with and married. His six-foot, 260-pound frame belied the gentle stillness within his heart. He'd been reared in a religious home that stressed church attendance, but not relationship with Christ. At first, he saw no need to change the direction of his life. But something in Anita and my mother made him begin to take notice of that part in him that was missing—intimacy with the Shepherd that carried my family through crises, as well as day-to-day living. He'd always just done it on his own, and his limited knowledge of Jesus had been fine for him. He began to watch, ask questions, and look at a book foreign to him—the Bible. A hunger grew inside him with each day.

After a few months, he called my sister from work. "It tingles, doesn't it?" he asked.

She sat for a few seconds trying to understand. "What tingles?"

"When you become born again, it tingles, doesn't it?"

She smiled on the other end of the phone. "Did you get saved?"

She could imagine his smile and nod. "Yeah." She heard a quiver in his voice as he told her about praying the sinner's prayer in his office during his break. When he did, something changed inside him. He became a sheep who belonged to the Shepherd. He wanted to please the Shepherd and began a deep, intense love relationship with Him as he entered the first gate of his journey.

HIS TOOLS

To bring them into their potential, the shepherd uses two tools to work with his sheep—a rod and staff (see Ps. 23:4). The rod is used for rescue, safety, and rodding—a practice where the shepherd places his rod across the sheep's backs and numbers those coming inside the fold so he can keep track of his charges (see Lev. 27:32).[10] Ezekiel says sheep will *"pass under the rod, and* [the shepherd] *will bring* [them] *into the bond of the covenant"* (Ezek. 20:37). By rodding, the shepherd knows exactly how many sheep he has and where each one is. Then he lies in front of the opening of the fold and literally becomes the gate to keep them from wandering off once they've been counted. God uses the same type of "rodding," too, as He keeps track of and counts His sheep, for His will is that not even *"one of these little ones should perish"* (Matt. 18:14). Our great Shepherd knows where we are on each step of our journey and personally protects us from whatever could befall us, even if the danger is from ourselves. Not only does He want us to go into the fold, but He also wants us to stay there and so provides safeguards to ensure we won't wander off: a Scripture that speaks to us, a dream to warn us, a "feeling" that something's wrong, a brother or sister who comes on the scene to encourage. Knowing our Shepherd discerns exactly where we are and cares that we won't wander off and be lost is comforting and encouraging. He's intimately familiar with every situation that concerns us, for *"the very hairs of* [our] *head are all numbered"* (Matt. 10:30). The minutiae of our lives matter to Him.

A crook, or staff, is used as a club to protect or correct sheep. Because the shepherd cares for them so much, he often must discipline them until they're brought into alignment with his will. We do the same with our own children because we don't want them to grow up with traits that would negatively impact them as adults. God cares for us enough that He wants us to be free from issues that plague us, so He, too, chastens us (see Heb. 12:6). That punishment isn't always easy. When a sheep has a habit of wandering off, sometimes the shepherd must break its legs. Although the punishment may seem harsh, if the shepherd allows a sheep to go its own way, it will become prey to all manner of dangers. The goal is for the sheep to line up with the shepherd's plan: *"For ye were as sheep going astray; but are now returned to the Shepherd and Bishop of your souls"* (1 Pet. 2:25). When we realize the Shepherd has only our best in mind, our mindset changes. Even though we all have issues, He steadfastly loves us.

JUST AS WE ARE

The Shepherd wants us just as we are with all our bumps, lumps, and foibles—and then He does a work in us in His way. I've seen that firsthand in my family. My nephew Chuck married Alice, his high school sweetheart. They had a full, rich life together: they traveled and had lots of amazing experiences until they finally settled down. She had it all: a law degree, a baby, and a husband she adored. Neither Alice nor Chuck was a Christian, however, and over the years, they adamantly argued that God's plan of salvation didn't make sense because so many "good" people weren't going to Heaven. For a long time, I avoided this discussion because they both vehemently questioned salvation—until one winter Sunday.

We'd canceled services where we pastored at our country church because of a snowstorm with drifts that made those narrow roads impassable. My sister Suzy called that morning and said Alice was coming to visit in the afternoon. I wanted to see her desperately because that week she'd learned she had colorectal cancer and was given a short time to live. The main roads to my sister's house had been cleared, so

Wade and I went down with one goal in mind—to tell Alice about her need for the Lord.

She listened politely and sat quietly as I finished. I was anticipating her usual liberal comments about the plan of salvation I'd laid out, but she said nothing. A few moments of silence were followed by her simple, quiet question: "If I turn to the Lord now, wouldn't it be self-serving like people who have jailhouse conversions?"

I smiled at her and shook my head. "Alice, He wants you any way He can get you, so He'll take your adversities and woo you...an arrest, a divorce, even cancer. He wants *you* just as you are."

She looked me straight in the eye, then nodded. That morning, she prayed the sinner's prayer with Wade and me in my sister's basement. The next few months she was on fire and hungry for the Lord, learning each day new ways to love Jesus. She'd found the Shepherd, the one she'd unknowingly longed for during the years she'd already spent on earth. She lived nearly a year after that, despite many prayers for her complete healing. But the most important thing Alice needed, her soul's healing, was accomplished before she went home to be with the Shepherd she'd grown to love.

He just wants us, whether we've never known Him or have fallen away. Isaiah says, *"All we like sheep have gone astray; we have turned every one to his own way; and the Lord hath laid on Him the iniquity of us all"* (Isa. 53:6). Though we were sinners, the Shepherd has taken all our transgressions upon Himself, and now we're free of sin and liberated to be His sheep. That doesn't mean, however, we won't still experience times when we get caught up in something of which our Father disapproves. When we stray, the Shepherd cares about our restoration. In Matthew 18:10-14, Jesus says lambs are so important that even if a man has 100 sheep, he'll leave the other 99 to find that one (see Matt. 18:12). God sent His Son to earth for one purpose: *"to save that which was lost"* (Matt. 18:11)—you, me, Alice. Before we became His sheep, our Shepherd loved us enough to die for us. Now as He watches over us, He gives whatever we need to become the sheep He created us to be.

CONCLUSION

When a baby is born, his daddy holds him in his arms and knows he's all potential. His son will be a nuclear physicist, a prize-winning author, or a star NFL quarterback. Even as he dreams for his son, though, he realizes his destiny will come through many years, hard work, tears, and smiles. For right now, that baby can do nothing. He can't raise his head or hold open his eyes or roll over by himself. Soon he will turn at his mommy's voice, discover his own hands, and begin to coo. His daddy will have high expectations for him throughout his life, but that will come one skill, one discovery at a time. For now, he's a new creation ready to be filled with knowledge and love from the daddy who hugs him to his breast.

The Sheep Gate is the starting point in this journey God has prepared for us. Jesus' death and resurrection and all that entitles us to, are the beginning, middle, and end of our walk. The Sheep Gate brings forgiveness into our lives through the blood of the Lamb and the grace of God. Here, we fall in love with our Shepherd, learn to rely on Him, and gain confidence that comes with His protection and relationship. This gate is our first encounter in Christian life; it's where we come to know Jesus, our sacrificial Lamb and our tender, loving Shepherd. We become set apart as His, so we can know His voice and do His bidding.

I love the words to the old nursery rhyme, "Mary Had a Little Lamb":

> "Why does the lamb love Mary so?"
> The eager children cry;
> "Why, Mary loves the lamb, you know,"
> The teacher did reply.[11]

It's a two-way relationship: the love of the Shepherd for the sheep and the love of the sheep for the Shepherd. Why do the sheep love the Shepherd so? It's simple! Because the Shepherd loves the sheep so thoroughly. When the world sees us, they see just sheep: smelly, dirty, dumb, ugly. When the Shepherd looks at us, He sees His wonderful creations and the potential we possess. Knowing the Shepherd and learning to love Him fosters a significant connection to Him. Our Shepherd is in control, for *"know ye that the Lord He is God: it is He that hath made us...we are His people, and the sheep of His pasture"* (Ps. 100:3). We don't need to do anything to earn entry into this gate. After we turn our lives over to Him, we just need to be His sheep and learn from Him and about Him. Our time here with our Shepherd builds a lifelong love affair.

CHAPTER

2

THE FISH GATE: SHARING THE NEWS

But the fish gate did the sons of Hassenaah build, who also laid the beams thereof, and set up the doors thereof, the locks thereof, and the bars thereof (Nehemiah 3:3).

Do you recall how excited you were when you first met your spouse? Remember how his voice thrilled you? Did the smell of his cologne or the anticipation of being with him make you smile whenever your thoughts wandered to him? I remember when my husband and I began to date—I'd be giddy whenever the phone rang. Most couples experience that time of excitement that comes with being involved in a new relationship.

In the same way, when we first become Christians, we're filled with wonder about what's transpired in our lives, so we can't wait to tell everyone about what we've discovered. We try, often successfully, to win others to God through our fervor and persistence. As new Christians, we learned at the Sheep Gate that Jesus, our Shepherd, died for our sins. Naturally, this revelation generated such excitement we wanted to tell others. That's why Nehemiah places the Fish Gate so close to the Sheep Gate.

THE FISH GATE

After going through the Sheep Gate and finding salvation, the next gate we must walk through is the Fish Gate. On the north wall, it was called the Fish Gate because fishermen sold their catches here. In our Christian walk, this gate represents our job to evangelize the lost and to bring catches of souls into God's Kingdom. When Jesus gave His disciples the call to *"come ye after Me, and I will make you to become fishers of men"* (Mark 1:17), the assignment was for us, too. Believers saved fewer than two years win most converts to God. Young Christians operate fluently in this gate because they still retain that initial wonder of the cross.

This gate was rebuilt by the sons of *Hassenaah* (meaning "to prick, thorny").[1] When God calls us to salvation, He pricks at our conscience to give our hearts to Him. Now, as fishermen, we pull others toward Him and let them feel the sting of God's drawing, too. When Jesus came to Saul on the road to Damascus, He said, *"I am Jesus whom thou persecutest: it is hard for thee to kick against the pricks"* (Acts 9:5). Saul's heart was so affected that he turned 180 degrees from persecuting Jesus' followers to being one of His chief supporters. This tugging of the heart is described again on the day of Pentecost. When Holy Spirit was given, Peter stood up, preached to the multitude, and proclaimed Jesus was Lord. As a result, *"when* [the people] *heard this, they were pricked in their heart, and said unto Peter and to the rest of the apostles, Men and brethren, what shall we do?"* (Acts 2:37). This pricking caused a change in these men, just as it did in each of us. Not only are sinners' hearts pricked for salvation, but also a Christian's heart can be pricked to action to promote Jesus as Lord to the lost.

HISTORY OF SYMBOLISM

The fish symbol has been important for Christians since the first century. For early Christians, the word for fish was the Greek word *ICHTHUS* (spelled in Greek, ΙΧΘΥΣ). *Ichthus* functioned as an acronym, with each "letter" standing for words that read, "Jesus Christ, Son of God, Savior."[2] Followers of Christianity were called *Pisciculi*, a Latin word formed from a root that means "fish."[3] During this time when disciples were winning converts to the risen Christ, persecutions against Christians began, so meetings were often secretive. Disciples drew the sign of a fish to identify themselves to other Christians. Often when they met, one would draw half a fish, and then his companion drew the other half to identify himself. They would also mark meeting places with this symbol, which is still part of Christian culture today.[4]

PERSECUTION

Although disciples brought in a lot of converts after Jesus' death, the secretive sign came into use by necessity. This was a perilous time for early believers, whose lives were threatened because of their beliefs. As they were persecuted, many scattered from Jerusalem to other places to avoid torture or death. God, however, used this persecution to spread the Gospel to different locations. Thriving churches sprang up in many areas: Rome, Antioch, Syria, and others. Cities were converted as a result of disciples fleeing persecution and fishing for converts wherever they landed.

As new converts, we often encounter persecution about our commitment. Some people don't understand why our lives have changed, so we meet with ridicule, derision, and exclusion. Though we have a human desire to be accepted, we cannot be if we're a separated people. As a former high school teacher, I saw teens teased because they followed convictions and wore only skirts or didn't cut their hair. Other kids would ask why some brought Bibles to school. Some were taunted for praying before lunch. Ridicule isn't new for Christians. Jesus was persecuted, and He warned that the world would hate us, so part of our growth needs to be understanding that we don't fit in anymore with the people and life we left behind (see John 15:19). We must look ahead. As we evangelize for souls, our commitment makes us understand that any cost is worth what we gain.

Persecution in our lives will continue, just as it did in the early disciples' time. When Christianity didn't subside on its own, church and political leaders decided to intensify efforts to crush it. Claudius, the first recorded Roman emperor to deal with Christians, issued an edict to banish the controversial religion from the Roman Empire[5]. After Christians remained, around a.d. 64, Nero began his abuse and brutally harassed, persecuted, and tortured them to worship Roman gods and deny Christ. Usually they died rather than renounce Jesus. Nero's motivations are unclear, but he was spurred on either by hatred, a desire to expel them from Rome, or a need for a scapegoat to deal with criticism of him for Rome's burning. Under his rule, Christians were arrested, mocked, and condemned in large numbers. Their executions were atrocious: they were dressed in animal skins so dogs could tear them apart or they were burned as human torches.[6]

About a generation later, Domitian had mass executions; and after him, though Trajan didn't actively pursue finding Christians, he banned their meetings and punished those who practiced the religion. Around a.d. 177, Marcus Aurelius, an emperor with intense hatred for Christians, continued the persecution with bloody, vicious punishments. Then, as the Christian population grew, so did tolerance for them. However, in a.d. 303, Emperor Diocletion and his successor Galerius renewed persecution and purging of Christians.[7] Some lost their lives while others lost property. Christians didn't lose their vision, though, to pursue this salvation Jesus had died for.

This time in history was costly for Christians. Estimates vary on the death toll from as few as under 2,000 to as many as 100,000.[8] The persecution didn't kill the movement, though. By the time Constantine became emperor in a.d. 337, it's estimated that 15 to 60 million people in the Roman Empire were Christians.[9] Early Christians are our model for how not only to withstand but also to flourish. Persecution continues on varied levels around the world today, yet Christianity continues despite it. Even as Americans we are often mocked and criticized by the media, in political forums, and even by those we're closest to. Once we become a friend of God, we're an enemy of satan—and he pulls out all stops to make us turn back. When we purpose to go full steam ahead for God, we put that enemy under our feet, though.

FISHERS OF MEN

The excitement of the new believer and the perseverance of the first century saints should be a model to those of us who have been Christians for a while. We can learn from them. Sometimes we become jaded and forget that showing the lost into the Sheep Gate is a commandment for us all. We should treat the sinner as if his soul were a precious commodity to be caught for the Kingdom. Just as God is not willing for any of His sheep to be lost, He also is *"not willing that any* [fish] *should perish"* (2 Pet. 3:9). Sometimes, just as in our marriages, we need to get excited again about salvation and remember God loves the lost just as much as He loves us. As a matter of fact, the unsaved are so important to Him that He gave His Son for the sinner. Fishing matters to God.

My Grandpa Sampson was a fishing fool. He went so often, and it sounded like such fun, I pleaded frequently with him to take me until he finally acquiesced. My brother Phillip and I rode with him after church one Sunday to experience firsthand this wonder. That day, I bounded from the car, pole in hand, and found a branch reaching out over the lazy Pipe Creek near Metamora, Indiana. I settled in to experience a day of Gramps' exciting passion. Was I in for a disappointment! The sitting was boring; the branch was hard; the mosquitoes loved my blood; the worms were slimy; and the hooks hurt, especially when they got caught in my hair. I complained so often that Gramps cut our excursion short to get rid of me.

That day, I was like most of us who are called as fishers of men. We just don't like to do it. Though all of us are commissioned to fish for converts, many of us see it as an inconvenience and not "our thing." Others, like Gramps, use every opportunity to fulfill that enormous task that seems less like a responsibility than a delight. This gate fosters that zeal.

From the beginning, disciples were called to be fishers of men. Despite the cost, they gladly chose to fish for converts to Jesus' life-changing salvation. In Acts, God sent Ananias to tell Saul he was a *"chosen vessel...*[who] *must suffer* [great things] *for* [God's] *name's sake"* (Acts 9:15-16). Ananias shared this with Saul, a former persecutor of the early church. Even though Saul understood the cost, he chose to spread the Gospel of Christ anyway. During his two missionary trips, he was mocked, persecuted, imprisoned, and nearly killed, but all this he considered as less important than his role of fisherman for souls. Are we as diligent when we know that our commitment to souls exacts a cost? Is the chance that we're mocked or rejected worth a soul?

My cousin used to come and stay with us frequently when we were young. He was nearly as old as Dad and slightly mentally impaired. He lacked good hygiene, pronounced words funny, and exuded a laugh that made the rest of us double up. He was named William, but everyone called him Pee Wee. He was notorious all around Central and Southeastern Indiana mostly for one reason—hitchhiking. In rhythm to his long stride, his head bobbed up and down as he trekked the roads between Franklin County and Indianapolis, walking, singing, and strumming his guitar painted with black acrylic and adorned in crudely shaped, bright-red letters announcing, "Wm. A. Hunter, Jesus is Real." For about anyone around, Pee Wee's name brought on stories of his escapades, and he bore the brunt of many a joke, including some from my young siblings and me. When I would meet someone for the first time, I got used to the question, "Uh, Hunter. You related to Pee Wee?" I would roll my eyes and nod as if it were my great burden to bear.

Years passed. I grew up, had a family, and rarely saw Pee Wee after he moved to Indianapolis and married. Then, one Saturday out of the blue, he came to stay all night with me and go to a "'vival meetin'." My teenaged daughters and their friends shared knowing glances and furtive smiles as Pee Wee sat on the living room couch and rambled on about things we could barely discern. I sat for a while and stifled grins myself before I went upstairs to get ready for church. Suddenly, I heard quick running on the stairs, and then Jennifer came racing in.

"Mom, Pee Wee's on the porch trying to get Elaine's mom saved." I cringed. Her mother was fairly well-to-do, and I knew from Elaine's conversations that she didn't believe as we did. I raced downstairs to the porch to try to defuse the situation.

As I bounded out the door, I saw her sitting on the brick rail along the front. Pee Wee was in front of her, facing her with his finger pointed close to her face. I gave her an "I'm so very sorry look," and she returned an "I understand completely" glance. She listened politely to what he was saying while I sat on the edge of one of my metal, antique lawn chairs and rocked slightly while he gave her his sinners' message. The longer I sat, though, the less mortified I became as a realization dawned on me. The shame for what was happening on the porch wasn't on Connie's not-quite-right cousin Pee Wee. The shame was on Pee Wee's not-quite-right cousin Connie.

In all the years I'd known this woman, never had *I* given her the message about a carpenter who gave His life for her. Never had *I* told her Jesus loved her and wanted her to spend eternity with Him. Never had *I* gotten beyond my societal norms to the place where I could let her know that God loved her as much as He loved me. Never had *I* loved her enough to tell her she should be born again. That day, I dropped my head and listened as Pee Wee unashamedly did my responsibility. I realized then he was a much better person than I was. He didn't have the intelligence, breeding, education, or finances most of us have, but he used the resources he'd been given so much better. He took seriously the call to go into the world to fish for souls. I sat and realized it was a simple thing to do, and I did it badly. When she left, I just hugged him and knew I had a lot to learn from him. From that day on, I was proud to say, "Yep, Pee Wee's my first cousin."

Because He loves the lost so much, the Lord asks us to share Him with others. Are we still following that directive? In Matthew 4:19, Jesus said, *"Follow Me, and I will make you fishers of men."* When we follow Him, being a fisher is a sure thing. He commanded His disciples to go to all nations and baptize them in the name of the Father, Son, and Holy Spirit (see Matt. 28:19-20). This Great Commission still rings true today, but are we doing that? Have we become one of those people who've forgotten Jesus' commandments? Are we fishing? Churches build all kinds of beautiful facilities and elaborate programs for fishing, but most don't ever go fishing. Sometimes fish wander into church ponds and someone might catch them, but most churches and Christians don't actually fish in the world's waters.

God gave man dominion over the fish of the sea in the first biblical reference to fish in Genesis 1:26. We still have dominion to bring fish to

Him and obey His charge: *"Go ye into all the world, and preach the gospel to every creature"* (Mark 16:15). In Matthew 13:47-50, Jesus compared the Kingdom of Heaven to a net where different types of fish are caught together and then separated, good from evil. That's a perfect picture of salvation: a mixture of many types of people, some who choose to be born again and some who do not. Our job is to fish for all of them, give each the opportunity, then let God draw them in.

SPEAKING THEIR LANGUAGE

In His time, Jesus could speak about fish, and His followers understood. He called seven fishermen as disciples, and He understood their culture. In Matthew 17:27, a fish provided taxes. In John 21:13, Jesus ate fish and bread with His disciples after He had risen; in Luke 24:42, it was fish and honeycomb. Through these and other occurrences involving fish, Jesus showed how others' needs mattered. Putting legs on our prayers draws others to Jesus. James 2:15-16 says,

> *If a brother or sister be naked, and destitute of daily food, and one of you say unto them, Depart in peace, be ye warmed and filled; [and] give them not those things...needful to the body; what doth it profit?*

If we can just show God's character to the lost, we do a lot to bring fish to Him. Just as the disciples had to leave their lives and livelihood to follow Jesus, we can't stay in our places of comfort and expect to find converts. We must step out and get to where the lost are to let them see how Christ will impact their lives.

Once, when my husband and I were pastoring, an acquaintance was having financial difficulties. We approached the church's Helping Hand, a food bank ministry, and gathered food and a check for the man's family. That night when we got home, Wade went to his house laden with those things. As the man looked at the check, he turned his head away to hide tears welling in his eyes. It was the same amount he needed the next day or his electricity was to be shut off. That event spoke a lot to him. Within a few months, he came to our home and gave his life to God. When Jesus meets people where their everyday crises are, His love demonstrates their need for that gentle Savior.

HOLY SPIRIT'S LEADING

Some probably feel inadequate to fish. In Luke 5:4-10, Jesus taught Peter and others sufficiency on Him by a lesson in fishing. They were experts but couldn't catch any during the night. When Jesus came on the scene and told them to cast to the boat's right side, their nets became so full they broke, and the boats nearly sank. This was so amazing to the men, Peter repented. Jesus used this lesson to teach them that *"henceforth thou shalt catch men"* (Luke 5:10). Like Peter's fishing experience, we're able to fish because Jesus is there with us and empowers us.

This is apparent in another story about fishing after Jesus' resurrection and Holy Spirit was sent. In John 21:6, Jesus appeared to them and again told them to cast their nets to the right side. This time, however, their nets didn't break; they caught 153 fish. The number 153 means "fruit bearing." Amazingly, 153 is "the product of 17 [elect of God or victory] x 9 [fruit of the Spirit] [and] the number of people Jesus ministers to in the Gospel of John."[10] In other words, when the elect of God (Christians) team with Holy Spirit, we can victoriously catch fish. The word ICHTHUS also gives us a clue to Holy Spirit's role in drawing the lost. Greek letters are assigned a numerical value. The letters in ICHTHUS not only mean "Jesus Christ, Son of God, Savior," but their combined numerical value also equals 1224, or 8 (resurrection, new beginnings) x 153 (fruit bearing).[11] We received a new beginning through Christ's resurrection as we found in the Sheep Gate. We combine that with Holy Spirit to bear fruit and to catch fish. This is how it will be when Holy Spirit nudges you to catch fish by His power.

Recently, I was in the beauty shop when a lady came in. She was on her way to the hospital where her infant granddaughter was seriously ill. Before she left, I prayed that they would be amazed at how that baby had improved. The report which came back was just that—her improvement that day was amazing. A couple weeks later I was in church and noticed that baby's young family a few rows ahead of me. It dawned on me that morning that nearly two years earlier I had gone for a loan at a bank where the young father had been the loan officer. We'd known him years before when he'd occasionally gone to the church we'd pastored, but he told me that day in the closing he hadn't been attending church for a while. Before I left, Holy Spirit led me to take his hand and pray for him to get stirred up again and find a place where he and his family could worship God together. That morning, two years later, I realized I was seeing the results of that Holy Spirit-led encounter that day in a room in the bank. After church, the young man made a point to come back and thank me for praying that day and said it had made a difference in bringing him and his family to the church they really enjoyed. I felt honored that God used me to pray for him then and for his daughter's healing now. When we let Holy Spirit direct, He knows exactly what will work each time.

Just as He did for us when we were born again and for this young man, God draws people to Himself through Holy Spirit, who enables us to show Christ's message. His grace demonstrates that He "[loves us] *with an everlasting love: therefore with loving-kindness* [has He] *drawn"* us (Jer. 31:3). *He* loves us, and *He* draws us. Many times the lost feel they're too bad for God to want them. Sinners should know God chooses to draw them despite their flaws. The message is simple—love! The key is for us to show that love by allowing Holy Spirit to do the work through us. Being obedient when He calls, whether in fishing for souls or moving on through the gates in our Christian experience, is the key to prosperity in all we do. Obedience is crucial. When we obey Holy Spirit's unction, He knows how to draw because He understands what that soul will relate to.

EVERYDAY FISHERMEN

Jesus was always aware of the importance of people's needs. When He fed the multitudes—5,000 (see Matt. 14:13-21) and 4,000 (see Matt. 15:32-38)—He demonstrated what fishing for men requires. In John 6, Jesus had a conversation with Philip about feeding the crowd. In John 6:9, when one disciple saw the meager amount of food, he asked, *"But what are they among so many?"* Jesus tells him that what is in their hands is sufficient to fish. With just five loaves and two fishes, they fed thousands and had leftovers. Jesus cared for them enough to want their physical needs taken care of as well as their spiritual ones. We must feel *agape* love for people, too, and make every soul important just as Jesus did. Though a sea of sinners abounds, we use God-given resources to catch one fish at a time; the Lord makes the increase. No one remembers what was said to the multitudes that day, but forever we remember what was done. People are won by our obedience and by showing God's love with what He places in our hands.

When my sister's four children were young, she was often the child-appointed taxi driver of other friends. Piling her four and the other strays that came along into her little yellow Chevette was difficult, and sometimes she resented doing others favors that were rarely reciprocated. But she continued. One boy in particular had moved from another state to live with a relative who refused to transport him to activities. By default, it once again fell to my sister. This boy was always polite and appreciative. He even showed his closeness to her family by later asking Suzy and her husband to stand with him when he was graduating and had no one to accompany him. She was glad she'd found a little extra space and gas money to make him feel like he had someone to turn to.

Then a few years after his graduation, she saw him at a church she was visiting. They exchanged their usual hugs and small talk. Later in the service, she was amazed when they announced that today's preacher would be that young man. As he spoke, he credited her family with showing him God's kindness when he was young. She'd never thought of trying to preach salvation to that little boy. She'd just lived her life in front of him like a Christian. She showed him love when others didn't and put herself out many times to prove he was worth the effort. Just as Jesus does. Through her, this young man had an introduction to a kind and giving way of life as alien to him as any foreign country, but he not only ultimately made his abode there, he now has a son who is following him into the ministry.

We often possess grand ideas about how we should go fishing. I remember during revivals as a child, preachers would urge us to commit our lives to God's will. I always did that and said, "God, have Your way in my life. I'm willing to do anything, but please don't ask me to be a missionary." When we think of that calling, we often visualize dire situations in deepest, darkest jungles with headhunters and cannibals. The truth is we can bring people we touch every day to the Lord. The old cliché is that our lives are the best Bible anyone can read. How true that is! Our conduct lets others see that a Christian is truly a separated being with a life that makes the lost want what we have. In the grocery, at work, in our neighborhood, even in our own home, we come across people we can lead to the Lord.

One day, I was at a yard sale when I heard a lady complain about her back hurting. Later, I saw her wince from pain. I followed her to the car and asked if she wanted prayer. When she agreed, I took her hand and prayed a simple prayer of faith. Shortly thereafter, at another yard sale, I saw her again. She told me her back was already better. By feeling the touch of God, she had an experience that impacted her in a way that let her see God's love. I don't know if my fishing brought her into the Kingdom, but it planted a seed. Often we're only the beginning of the process of someone else coming to God, but our part is important when Holy Spirit moves on us. He knows exactly how to speak to someone so he or she will understand.

SIGNS AND WONDERS

Allowing Holy Spirit to do signs and wonders also draws people. In Acts 3 at the Gate Beautiful, Peter and John healed the lame man. This healing in itself was miraculous until Acts 4 tells the results of that healing. Because of that incident, *many of them which heard the word believed; and the number of the men was about five thousand"* who were saved (Acts 4:4). The same occurred in Acts 9. Peter told Aeneas to rise and make his bed. When he arose, *"all that dwelt at Lydda and Saron saw him, and turned to the Lord"* (Acts 9:35). Peter and John obeyed the Lord, He brought the increase; and two entire towns were saved.

This is how my heathen family came to God, too. In 1952, my aunt was told she would die when she was 16. However, when my grandfather took her to a faith healer, she was delivered. That event turned my entire family to the Lord because it spoke to them of a God who loved them enough to spare their sister/daughter and let her live to see her great-grandchildren. My grandfather's and parents' conversion changed not only their destinies but also those of every other generation to come.

Jesus also caught fish through prophetic actions. One example of the drawing of Holy Spirit involves a word of knowledge. Nathanael and Philip had been talking about Jesus whom Nathanael so adamantly opposed that he asked, *"Can there any good thing come out of Nazareth?"* (John 1:46). Later, when Jesus arrived, He said to Nathanael, *"Before that Philip called thee, when thou wast under the fig tree, I saw thee"* (John 1:48). Because of this simple prophetic announcement, Nathanael exclaimed, *"Rabbi, Thou art the Son of God...the King of Israel"* (John 1:49). Words of knowledge speak to the unsaved about God's love. They say that God is not only real but also that He sees them and cares about them. As fishers of men, we can let acts of Holy Spirit be the ultimate drawing.

A word of knowledge made the difference once when Wade and I were doing missionary work in Mexico. One Saturday, Bob, a wonderful elderly gentleman, took us and an interpreter to a border town to minister at a family's house. Only about four or five people were there that day, but one was a little girl. God impressed me she had something wrong with her hearing. When that was verified, we prayed, and she received perfect hearing instantly. She was so excited that she made me a bracelet and sheepishly brought it to me. We left and scheduled a meeting for the next Saturday at another house a few streets away. When we got there, many people had come because they'd heard the story of the little girl's healing. We ministered that day for over six straight hours as they sent for more and more people to come and hear us. From this one miracle, many were healed and saved that day. After we left and went back to Indiana, Bob ended up baptizing 80 people—in a horse trough. Holy Spirit's ability tells people He's real, and that's the greatest sermon we can ever preach at the Fish Gate.

CONCLUSION

When I went fishing with Gramps that day, the guys brought home several fish. We took "our" fish back to his house, and I got to see my grandfather scale, debone, and fillet those fish quickly and professionally. As I scrunched up my nose at the smell and horror of fish guts, Gramps cooked a wonderful feast. We aren't responsible for cleaning up the fish we win for God. If we catch them, He'll clean them. Even in little bitty Pipe Creek we found plenty of fish—and masses exist wherever you are. Ezekiel 47:9 says, *"it shall come to pass...there shall be a very great multitude of fish...and every thing shall live whither the river cometh."* Not only the world's rivers, but also your city, your neighborhood, your street, your job, and maybe your home are filled with fish needing to be caught. One at a time.

As we share the Lord with others, we, too, grow in Him. Our obedience, love, sensitivity to Holy Spirit, and understanding of God become more fine-tuned. Recently, I heard a song that asks, "What if I'm 15?"[12] The lyrics' premise is that we need to be diligent about spreading the word about Jesus' love because it may take many years and 15 encounters for someone to understand his or her need for the Savior. And what if I'm that 15th encounter? What if the difference between Heaven and hell was getting past myself and caring enough about others to want them to spend eternity with a loving Father? The Fish Gate reminds us of the importance of evangelism and servanthood. Our Christian walk isn't meant to be only self-serving: it's to be lived for others. Whether our concern is with another's salvation or just being a servant to help him or her, we learn early on that a Christian is made to give. Just like Jesus.

CHAPTER

3

THE OLD GATE: GOING DEEPER

Moreover the old gate repaired Jehoiada the son of Paseah, and Meshullam the son of Besodeiah; they laid the beams thereof, and set up the doors thereof, and the locks thereof, and the bars thereof (Nehemiah 3:6).

During my 33 years as a high school English teacher, quite a few new teachers came and went. Many began their teaching careers thinking they'd already learned everything they needed to and that those of us who'd been there for a while were out of the loop about what works "now" with students. One first-year teacher challenged me about a writing model I used with my kids.

"I just got out of college," she remarked. "That style of writing would never work there."

"I used it when I was in college. It worked fine even for my master's."

"Well, that was a long time ago. It doesn't work now."

I just walked away. She was often quick with challenges about other teachers' ways, too. This went on for a couple of years until she came to me one day seeking my notes for how to teach the writing style she'd belittled before. Over the years similar scenarios were repeated with other new teachers who grew to realize that what they'd learned in college was only the foundation for real education. We can read textbooks and listen to professors, but when we actually get in front of a class we must discipline as well as teach, we realize what we really don't know and seek help from others who are more seasoned. So it is with our Christian walk.

When we become Christians, we think we've learned the only message necessary: Jesus died for our sins so we can go to Heaven. What a beautiful lesson to get into our spirits! After a while, as we become more mature in God, we realize that our initial knowledge of God is just a speck on the tip of the iceberg. We learn that our walk can be as deep as we want to take it. Though the plan of salvation is so easy that even a fool can walk on that road and not err (see Isa. 35:8), in order to grow in God, we need to understand the deeper things He has to offer.

THE OLD GATE

We came through the Sheep and Fish Gates and learned the basics; now we're ready to grow in the Old Gate, sometimes called the Jeshanah Gate. This gate was the main entrance to the city at the north side and apparently got its name because the road which ended there came from the town of Jeshanah, meaning "old" (see 2 Chron. 13:19).[1] For a Christian, the Old Gate represents the phase in our walk where we learn God's old ways and truths, which are rock-solid. Here, we experience our first substantial growth in Him because now we must decide how seriously we want to know Him. The love we gained for the Shepherd in the Sheep Gate grows even stronger as we learn about Him, cultivate a love for His Word, and find how to do things His way. This is a crucial phase if we're to grow in the Lord.

The Old Gate was repaired by *Jehoiada,* meaning "knowledge of the Lord."[2] Getting to know the Lord is what this gate is all about. Jehoiada was the son of *Paseah,* which means "passing over," which is what we're doing now—passing over into a deeper phase in God.[3] *Meshullam,* meaning "peaceable; perfect," also repaired the gate.[4] Truly, God's ways are perfect, and in this gate, we gain more trust in His ways. Meshullam was the son of *Besodeiah,* "the counsel of the Lord," which is the gate's purpose—to get to know God's wisdom and counsel.[5] The Old Gate is next in the progression of gates for a reason: we're "passing over" into a new phase in spiritual maturity as we learn God's perfection.

His ways have flourished for all of time, and we need to know them. Psalm 93:2 says, *"Thy throne is established of old: Thou art from everlasting."* He was from the beginning—yet when we get to know the Lord, we often don't take advantage of what our forefathers knew about Him. People say our ceiling should be the next generation's floor; instead, we often "reinvent the wheel." For example, when I was a child, it was common in services to "pray it through," "wait on the Lord," or "fall on your face," but many today haven't experienced concepts basic to the previous generation's walk with God. If we spend time in this gate, we'll learn much of our Lord, especially from those who've already experienced Him.

LEVELS OF CHRISTIAN MATURITY

Just as in a person's natural development, various levels occur in everyone's walk with God—from infancy to adulthood. First John 2:12-13 says,

I write unto you, little children, because your sins are forgiven you for His name's sake. I write unto you, fathers, because ye have known Him that is from the beginning. I write unto you, young men, because ye have overcome the wicked one....

Since each group has different needs for development, we should go through this gate at every level. As children, we learn of the Lord, read His Word diligently, and are open to being directed in the right path. As older Christians, our experiences are valuable for mentoring others in God's ways. We come into this gate first as sheep, but at some point we must become a shepherd to those who can benefit from our experiences with God. Our trip around the gates can help us and others who are both mentors and mentees.

As teens, or "young men," as John called us, we see Him from a more adult, yet not fully mature perspective. Teen Christians are often like regular teenagers. They think they know more than they actually do, so they end up having a harder time because they neglect to listen to those God has put into their lives to help them. The bottom line is that "those who cannot remember the past are condemned to repeat it."[6] Christian teens have little experience to draw from but think they have everything already figured out. Just as our own teens must develop a moral compass, so Christian teens must know God's ways in order to grow into His fullness and their destinies as men and women of God. Often that guidance comes from more seasoned Christians.

It seemed as if overnight my lovely, kind, obedient daughters became people I didn't even recognize: teens! Suddenly they knew everything. I wasn't smart enough to help them with homework—even English, my major. I couldn't advise them because I was too out-of-the-loop. My very existence was an embarrassment, and they constantly found ways to inform me I would forever scar them with my outdated clothes; old-lady hairstyle; mannerisms; and, Heaven forbid, dancing or singing style.

Once, when they were in high school, much to their horror, I dressed for Hippie Day during Homecoming Spirit Week at school. When I came downstairs, Jill was sitting at the kitchen table eating breakfast.

"Mom," she said, her mouth snapping open, eyes reflecting disbelief, and head shaking vehemently. "Please don't wear that today!"

"Why not? It's Hippie Day. I'm a hippie." I slid my John Lennon glasses lower on my nose as I smiled sweetly at her.

"You're not funny. Everyone will see you." I just laughed and gave her a raised-eyebrow, that's-kinda-the-point smile. She leered at me for a couple seconds then turned back to her food. "Besides, that's not how hippies dressed, anyway!" she said curtly.

"Well, Jill," I said, "I've sorta been there, done that. How do *you* know how they're supposed to dress?"

She just looked at me with her "duh" eyes. "Mom, I saw how Jenny dressed on *Forrest Gump!*" Like natural teens, less mature Christians often don't understand that older Christians have not only read it, heard it, and seen it, but have lived it and have a wealth of information to share.

Whichever group we're in, we must either learn or remember what God has done, and that happens in the Old Gate. When we came in as sheep, we knew nothing about God and what He had promised. Now, knowing His ways and how His Kingdom functions becomes critical. Kingdom principles exist, such as seedtime and harvest, that, when we understand them, give us promises and power. We can claim them as our godly inheritance if we know what they are and how to activate those principles. Equally important are covenant rights, privileges, and responsibilities occurring through Holy Spirit's power and secured by the authority of the name and blood of Jesus. Our rights are enumerated as we learn more of the Word. For immature Christians, those rights seem unattainable; but as we grow in God, we understand more of what He's given and how we can claim those things as ours.

MEMORIAL PILLARS

If we don't become acquainted with God on a personal level, how can we know what He'll do for us? Making memorial pillars is crucial so we understand what God has done in the past and know what He'll do in the future. When Israel was going into the Promised Land, Joshua set up pillars so they could remember what God had done on their behalf. In Joshua 4:6-7, God gives this instruction:

> ...When your children ask their fathers...What mean ye by these stones? Then ye shall answer them, That the waters of Jordan were cut off before the ark of the covenant...and these stones shall be for a memorial unto the children of Israel for ever.

Drawing on personal events where God intervened for us catalyzes our faith. Just as the Hebrews had their memories and rituals to celebrate God, my family had its own memorial pillars.

When I was a little girl, I often heard the story of Mrs. Johnson, a lady my mother became acquainted with after she was on a radio program similar to *Queen for a Day*. She had come on the show because she was dying of cancer and wanted to get a cow from the producers so that when she died, her children would have milk to drink. This story touched my mother's heart. Though my family lived in Ohio and Mrs.

Johnson was from the Carolinas, my mother felt led to help her. My parents had come into Christianity at the time of the '50s faith healers, so they already had erected many memorial pillars about what God could do. Though they were still young Christians, they understood the importance of trusting and obeying God, so my mother wrote the radio station and got Mrs. Johnson's address. Finally, after correspondence, Mom sent her a bus ticket, and she came to Ohio for prayer.

William Branham was holding a revival about 30 miles away in Connersville, Indiana. Mom drove Mrs. Johnson there, and they took their seats among the expectant crowd jammed into an outside amphitheater. The service started, and Brother Branham began to preach. He hadn't been speaking for very long when he stopped, motioned toward my mother and Mrs. Johnson in the stands, and said, "Someone sitting over here has cancer." He described her symptoms and her doctor's and nurse's appearances. Then he simply proclaimed she was healed. She was. She went back home, canned fruits and vegetables from the garden, and took care of her family.

After a few months, though, she called and said cancer symptoms had returned. Most people would have given up then and thought the healing was a fluke. However, my mother had her own memorial pillars about what God could do. She told Mrs. Johnson to refuse any return of cancer because God had given her a healing and wouldn't take it back. Mrs. Johnson clung to that and lived to see her grandchildren. Even though my mother was a young Christian herself, God used her to bring life because she'd spent time in the Old Gate and understood her Father's heart. That event became a memorial pillar not only to the Johnsons but also the Hunters.

David said, *"I will remember the works of the Lord: surely I will remember Thy wonders of old"* (Ps. 77:11). By remembering what God did years ago, we grow in faith to believe Him for what He'll do for us now. One night in a service, Jim came down front to help pray for others. I saw a vision of his back with a certain spot highlighted. His stepson was standing near him, so I told him to put his hands on Jim's back. When he did, it wasn't exactly where I had seen in the vision, so I told him where to put his hand. Unknown even to Jim's wife, he'd injured it that day in exactly the spot God had shown. He was instantly healed. That became a memorial pillar as Jim realized that God knew him and cared; he can cling to that memory when he needs God's touch again. The Old Gate is a time of remembering God's past works to give us assurance of what He can do now. Esther 9:28 says, *"These days should be remembered and kept throughout every generation, every family, every province, and every city… nor* [should] *the memorial of them perish from their seed."*

KNOWING GOD'S WAYS

The second reason the Old Gate is important is that we learn how to do things God's way. David said, *"Shew me Thy ways, O Lord; teach me Thy paths"* (Ps. 25:4). Sometimes doing things God's way is difficult. My mother wasn't one to give us kids pet names, but she called me "Hammerhead" because of my stubbornness. Even as an adult, I often want to do things my way even when God has shown me something else. Each time trouble plagues my life, it's because I've pursued my own direction, not God's. As new Christians, we don't yet understand God's manner of doing things. Though we possess the mind of Christ, getting that mind fine-tuned takes time. He's the Lord of all creation, and He chooses to accomplish things in a mode we sometimes don't understand. If the only thing we learn at this gate is just to obey and do it His way, we have mastered a great lesson.

We can know our parents with photographs and anecdotes. True intimacy, however, comes from spending time with them and learning about them firsthand. By the same token, the best way we can know God is to come into the Old Gate and be in His presence. As new creatures in the Sheep Gate, we learned and still are learning about the Shepherd and find that His depths are infinitesimal. In this gate, we learn more of this incomparable God who says, *"Remember the former things of old: for I am God, and there is none else…there is none like Me"* (Isa. 46:9). *Strong's* defines the word *old* in this Scripture as "everlasting, perpetual."[7] He is forever and solid; getting to know Him makes our lives more stable, too. We need to seek God through the Bible and become intimately acquainted with this "forever" God. Then we can know Him in His majesty for who He is.

Why is it important to know Him and His ways? This journey has just begun, and many twists and turns will happen along the way. Right now, just as we learned in the Sheep Gate, we need to understand that even if we don't see what He's doing in our lives, we must simply trust Him just like we trusted the Shepherd implicitly. In His time, in His way, He'll bring us into the place He has for us. Once Wade and I had been long awaiting God's answer to our life's direction. I was upstairs and felt Him saying, "Do you trust Me?" As I pondered His question, I knew that, although I had ideas about how I wanted our lives to go, I wanted His will and trusted Him with my life, my talents, my career, my children, my husband. No matter what, I trusted Him. I went downstairs and told Wade about what God had put into my heart. He got his laptop and began to read. While I was upstairs telling God I trusted Him, Wade was downstairs writing about the same thing. Because both of us affirmed our trust in Him that night, things began to fall into place that had been years in coming. Can you learn to trust?

GOD'S REDEMPTIVE NAMES

The concept of needing God to provide for various problems that arise isn't new to our times. He realized from the beginning we would need Him on every level, just like His children did in ancient times. When that hardship arose—healing, deliverance, provision—He revealed His identity to His children and they recognized His ability to provide that for them. Some names He became were:

- *Jehovah-Ropheka*—The Lord Our Healer (see Exod. 15:26). When God made the bitter waters sweet at Marah, He demonstrated Himself as the healer.

- *Jehovah-Shammah*—The Lord Is There (see Ezek. 48:35). God gave Ezekiel a revelation of the city He would someday inhabit.

- *Jehovah-Shalom*—The Lord Is Peace (see Judg. 6:24). God reassured Gideon after he'd seen the angel of the Lord.

- *Jehovah-Jireh*—The Lord Our Provider (in the mount of the Lord it shall be seen) (see Gen. 22:14). Abraham called the place this when God provided a sacrifice instead of Isaac.

- *Jehovah-Nissi*—The Lord Our Banner (see Exod. 17:15). Moses built an altar to the God who defeated Amalek through Joshua after Aaron and Hur held up his hands so the rod could be raised.

- *Jehovah-Tsidkenu*—The Lord our Righteousness (see Jer. 23:6). The prophet foretold of Jesus' coming when God would raise a branch who would be righteous.

- *Jehovah-Mekaddishkem*—The Lord That Doth Sanctify You (see Exod. 31:13). God told Moses to keep the Sabbath as a sign that He was the God of sanctification.

- *Jehovah-Rohi*—The Lord Our Shepherd (see Ps. 23:1). David proclaims God as the great Shepherd who cares for His flock.

As we continue our Christian journey, we know that whatever issues crop up, His character covers those needs. When we need provision, we rely on *Jehovah-Jireh*; when we need peace, *Jehovah Shalom*. He's what we need, when we need it. This God has been around perpetually and will continue to be, demonstrating Himself for whatever situation we stumble into.

OUR HERITAGE

Another reason we should spend time in this gate is that as young Christians, we need to know our heritage rights from God. However, we also must know He has precepts we must fulfill in order for those promises to come to fruition. Exodus 15:26 says,

> *If thou wilt diligently hearken to the voice of the Lord...and wilt do that which is right in His sight...I will put none of these*

diseases upon thee, which I have brought upon the Egyptians:
for I am the Lord that healeth thee.

In other words, God rewards His children with freedom from things that plague the sinner *if* we listen to Him and obey. In this gate, we can assert our faith because as God's children we realize these things belong to us. He tells us to *"ask for the old paths...and walk therein, and ye shall find rest for your souls..."* (Jer. 6:16). Whatever we need—healing, peace, rest, or a multitude of other needs—this gate lets us know what God has given us and what our responsibility is if we want to claim it.

Additionally, we need to know how to avoid the pitfalls that some fall into. Job 22:15 asks if we've noted those routes that other men have taken that ended in devastation. When we listen to the exhortations of mentors or read the Word, we're less likely to fall prey to the fowler. We learn God is jealous and wants our full commitment to Him. Jeremiah 18:15, 17 says,

Because My people hath forgotten Me...and...stumble[d]...from
the ancient paths....I will scatter them...I will shew them the
back, and not the face, in the day of their calamity.

We fall out of our kingly position when we don't observe His ways. Following God's will, however, makes us the head and not the tail (see Deut 28:13). Sometimes a child learns by touching the stove instead of being warned about it—but at this gate, if we take the advice of those who have worn a path to God's heart, we can avoid such consequences. We don't have to suffer the burns and scars our choices will bring. In this gate, we learn that what we don't do is often as important as what we actually do.

MENTORS

In the Old Gate, we also discover that Christian mentors can help guide us through rough areas. When Rehoboam became king, he sought advisers about dealing with his subjects. However, he didn't accept the wisdom of older, wiser men, but looked toward those less seasoned (see 1 Kings 12:6,8,13). Because he didn't heed counsel of veterans, but followed advice of younger men with ulterior motives, he had to flee his kingdom and brought rebellion against David's house forever (see 1 Kings 12:19).

Like Rehoboam, whether we're young or old Christians, at times we need advice. At the Old Gate we learn from the successes and failures of those who went before us. We make choices not only for ourselves but also for our families; those decisions can follow our children and grandchildren just as Rehoboam's choices impacted his posterity forever. We all like counsel with pleasing words, but often the best thing an adviser can do is be firm and offend our senses because eternity may be hanging in the balance (see Gal. 5:21). Godly mentors with direct words spoken in love can lead us to sustaining paths.

Even as Eli mentored Samuel to become the greatest judge in Israel's history, we all need mentors to help us grow in Him and in our destinies. In my childhood, we had a church family who looked out for us. One woman, a little Indian lady named Sister Manuel, showed us in many ways, both prophetically and personally, what it means to be a woman of faith. I've carried her guidance into my adult life. The Old Gate reminds us that older Christians occupy an important place in God's Kingdom:

> *When I am old and greyheaded, O God, forsake me not; until I have shewed Thy strength unto this generation, and Thy power to every one that is to come* (Psalm 71:18).

We have a responsibility to show who He is to those who are younger.

Often when we think of the old, we think of people slowing down and being "put out to pasture." That's not God's way, however, for He sees worth in us no matter where we are in our lives. The first reference to "old" is in Genesis 5:32 when Noah was 500 years old when he had his sons. Instead of a time of decreased productivity, this gate shows that even the old have fertility. So much has happened in previous generations; we sheep must learn about those things so that our confidence in God grows each day. Then, as we become mentors, we can pass that knowledge on to another generation. Like Noah, this gate is still a place of fertility even though we're old and gray.

At some point in our walk through the gates, we'll become seasoned Christians, and older men and women can teach those who are younger many things. Titus 2:3-5 reminds...

aged women...that they may teach the young women to be sober, to love their husbands, to love their children, to be discreet, chaste, keepers at home, good, obedient to their own husbands....

Here, in the Old Gate, young men and women look to us for marital advice, child-rearing tips, financial guidance, spiritual direction, and just about anything else that would allow them to live a godly, overcoming lifestyle. Isaiah 58:12 says we will *"raise up the foundations of many generations; and* [we] *shalt be called, The repairer of the breach, The restorer of paths to dwell in."* That puts a lot of responsibility on mentors, but when we were younger we learned at this gate from our own mentors, and now we can pass on that wisdom. As we traverse around the wall, we all need to come in through this gate several times, not only for ourselves but for others.

MAKING WAY FOR THE NEW

By teaching these things, we also learn that the name of the Lord endures *"for ever; and* [His] *memorial...throughout all generations"* (Ps. 135:13). God doesn't allow everything to stay the same, however. Once we have learned from the old, we can bring that into the new works God initiates. He wants a firm foundation for the new generation to accomplish His work which He's bringing in a new way. Therefore, He uses both groups to bring about something new: the older generation starts the work, but the newer often completes it. For example, David had the heart and vision for building the Lord's temple and gathered materials to build it, but his son Solomon actually constructed it. Eli taught Samuel, but Samuel became a great priest and judge. Moses brought God's people out of Egypt and through the wilderness, but Joshua took them into the Promised Land. The old man must be replaced by a new man, but the old must nurture the new so he may step into his place as the godly person he was created to be. If that doesn't happen, the next move of God may be doomed for failure because ill-equipped teens are doing a work they're not prepared for.

Matthew 13:52 says,

...every scribe which is instructed unto the kingdom of heaven is like unto a man that is an householder, which bringeth forth out of his treasure things new and old.

Both are important, and God's ways of bringing His purpose to fruition are often something never before experienced. Great moves of God like Azusa Street, the healing revivals of the '50s, or Charismatic Renewal movements of the '70s were extensions of prior moves of God that a new generation brought to fruition. Younger people need older ones to give them stability, but younger Christians often lead in movements. Though Jesus personally taught His disciples, much of the New Testament was written by men like Paul who learned from those who walked with Jesus. Older Christians pray, intercede, and teach younger Christians who in turn seek God diligently until they, too, know Him. Then they will *"eat* [of the] *old store, and bring forth the old because of the new"* (Lev. 26:10).

CONCLUSION

Mark Twain once said,

When I was a boy of 14, my father was so ignorant I could hardly stand to have the old man around. But when I got to be 21, I was astonished at how much the old man had learned in 7 years.[8]

Sometimes it's hard to think our spiritual fathers are a treasure chest of wisdom, but what they have to offer gives us priceless fodder for our maturation. The Old Gate represents solid growth, God's way, learned in large part through the Word and our mentors. It signifies mingling the old with the new to bring about God's purpose. As the new comes forth, the old will help it maintain balance. When new wine is being put into bottles, adding a little old wine allows it to ferment properly. By the same token, God's new move often has to be integrated with the old for it to come into the fullness He has planned. The Old Gate lets us move deeper into our walk by giving us the steadiness of the time-proven old while we become the new creation we are destined to be.

Nehemiah began his repair of the wall one brick at a time. By the same token, we grow in God and build our own house one step, one experience, at a time. As I wrote in the Prologue, to build a home, we have many choices: carpet color, tile layout, light fixtures. Though all these decisions are important, the home starts with a foundation. If that isn't solid, nothing else matters, for the house will look good but have no substance. The Old Gate lays that foundation for all other things to be added—as we get to know the Word, learn about Him, and create experiences that strengthen our faith. Then, we can grow sturdy and strong in Him while moving on toward our godly destinies.

CHAPTER

4

THE VALLEY GATE:
ENDURING THE TRIALS

And I went out by night by the gate of the valley, even before the dragon well, and to the dung port, and viewed the walls of Jerusalem, which were broken down, and the gates thereof were consumed with fire (Nehemiah 2:13).

The valley gate repaired Hanun, and the inhabitants of Zanoah; they built it, and set up the doors thereof, the locks thereof, and the bars thereof, and a thousand cubits on the wall unto the dung gate (Nehemiah 3:13).

Valleys! When you hear that word, you know exactly what happens at this stage in your Christian growth. Makes you wanna head for the hills, so to speak. Your car breaks down. Your unmarried daughter tells you she's pregnant. You lose your cell phone. Your husband says he doesn't love you anymore. Your coworker decides making your life miserable is part of his job description. Valleys happen, and how you maneuver through them makes you stronger, but that's little comfort when your whole world seems to be spiraling out of control.

Recently, we were leaving church when a young man caught up with us in the foyer. He fell into step beside us and without much small talk told us about the troubles going on in his life—financial issues, job insecurity, marital discord—everything hitting him hard. He said he couldn't understand why all that was happening to him.

"Has God forgotten me?" he questioned.

I had listened without comment, and then just smiled at him. "Of course not! As hard as this seems, one thing is certain. God has a plan for your life, and sometime you'll see how all these trials have worked into that plan."

The valley is a fact of life we don't want to think about, but it happens to all of us. God doesn't bring bad things on us—His Word says good things come from Him (see James 1:17). He uses tribulations, however, to refine our character. Last year we remodeled the kitchen in our nearly 100-year-old house. We thought it would be a simple process of putting down a floor, hanging new cabinets, and applying a fresh coat of paint. However, as we tackled one job, we found another needing repair that we hadn't anticipated. At the time, I was frustrated during the months we lived with a refrigerator in the dining room, a microwave as our only source of cooking, piles of cabinet items boxed everywhere, and drywall dust coating the entire house. Eventually, though, resolving these difficulties produced a kitchen we can be proud of. New drywall is more eye-pleasing than cracked plaster, and if some things we came across, like old wiring, had been ignored, we may have experienced trouble down the road. That's how it works for us with trials. They're not easy during the refining process, but they all work together to make us more like Him.

A friend of mine was married to a man who abused both her and her children. She'd married in a time when she felt women should stay in their marriages and few job opportunities afforded an uneducated woman a way out. She stayed with him despite what she endured. Several years after her children were adults, she told me she saw some good that came about through those terrible experiences. Even though the ordeal was painful in many ways, some of her children's good personality traits were a result of their hard, taskmaster dad: a solid work ethic, empathy, mechanical skills, and a wide range of knowledge on many topics. Difficult experiences shaped the characters of those children into the wonderful adults they grew to be.

THE VALLEY GATE

We're the same way with our trials. God uses experiences we go through—and some are really hard—to take aspects of our character and shape us. As I told the questioning young man, maybe He wants us to foster patience, kindness, gentleness, or humility. Trials produce what good times cannot. We came in the Sheep Gate, won souls at the Fish Gate, and got to know the Lord more at the Old Gate. God often gives us time in the first three gates so we can learn things that will help us endure our valleys. As we become more established, the Valley Gate is crucial for our growth. We cringe even to hear the word valley because we know what's to come: a rebellious child, financial problems, seemingly irresolvable decisions to make. Like it or not, this gate represents trials and tribulations we must go through during our journey with God. Many become Christians and think they'll experience trouble no more; that's far from the truth. Everyone on earth faces difficulties. We shouldn't, however, just go through them but rather grow through them.

A man named Hanun (gracious, merciful) and the inhabitants of Zanoah (forgetfulness, desertion) hung this gate.[1] Grace takes us through here in order to help us leave behind issues that brought us to this valley in the first place. We're traveling toward our Assignment Gate, so all things that stand in the way of that destiny must be eliminated during our journey. If you look at the Map of Jerusalem in Appendix 1, you'll see we stay in the Old Gate for a while before the Lord allows us to go into the Valley Gate, but eventually trials of the valley happen. God permits us to wait to go through this gate until we're more established because often this can seem overwhelming to us.

Sometimes, though, Christians experience the Valley Gate as soon as they walk into the Sheep Gate. The truth is that many valleys we encounter are satan's attempt to discourage us and get us to turn back—persecution, ridicule, or other issues. However, many trials we go through are simply consequences of our past decisions: divorce, jail, and illnesses. God can still change those things, but often He uses them for our ultimate good. In this gate God allows testing to bring us deeper in Him and in our reliance on Him. God's interested in our success, not our failure, so you can be sure that if you're in a valley, He'll not give you more than you can handle (see 1 Cor. 10:13).

RETURN TRIPS

The Valley Gate was the lowest point in Jerusalem's wall, just as it represents the depths in our Christian lives. By night, Nehemiah went through this gate, traveled around the city, then returned by the same gate (see Neh. 2:13-15). His journey mirrors our own. We go through the Valley Gate multiple times, depending on what God needs to accomplish in our character. Sometimes I find myself relearning something I thought I'd mastered long before. But there it is—looming large before me, just awaiting a valley experience. A lesson I've had to learn many times is to watch my mouth—whether I'm being reminded to pray with faith, speak positive words, or refrain from talking about others. Recently, I again became valley-bound as words I'd said came back to me. I had to learn that lesson all over again. As embarrassing as the experience was, the valley gave me renewed insight into the importance of watching what I say because God wants me to go into my assignment with that weakness conquered. Some people speak of the Valley Gate as "making another trip around the mountain"—in reference to the Hebrews' wilderness experiences. Despite God's patient efforts, most of the Israelites never learned the lesson for which their valley was designed and couldn't go into their destinies with Him.

This gate leads into Hinnom Valley, which connects to the Kidron Valley, east of the city, through which the Brook Kidron flows. This stream reminds me of two victorious valley experiences. When David was at one of his lowest points, he crossed the Kidron in despair (see 2 Sam. 15:23). His son Absalom had undermined him, betrayed him, then sought to kill him and take over his throne. Absalom had put together a following to pursue his father, and David was running for his life. When he went across the Kidron while fleeing from Absalom, he was not only trying to survive but also dealing with the betrayal of someone he loved, a sorrow greater than many can bear. David's experience is an example of a valley. However, his return trip across the Kidron was victorious against Absalom and his forces, and he regained his throne.

Jesus also crossed the Brook Kidron during a time of great trial—as He was going to Gethsemane. When He went across that stream into which Jerusalem's sewage flowed, He knew the ordeal He had to face at Calvary. Then, *"...He went forth with His disciples over the brook Cedron, where was a garden, into the which He entered, and His disciples"* (John 18:1). He was accompanied by apathetic friends during His trip across the Kidron to pray, despite His extreme emotions about the ordeal He was to experience. He even prayed He might forgo it. He was *"in an agony* [so] *He prayed more earnestly: and His sweat was as it were great drops of blood falling down to the ground"* (Luke 22:44). This physical state sometimes happens to prevent serious harm when we experience great stress. Jesus' grief was so intense that His blood vessels burst and blood was in His sweat. Since His suffering created this level of stress, this experience would qualify as a valley for Him. However, after Gethsemane, He returned in the victory of the cross. If both David and Jesus went through valleys and came out victorious, why shouldn't we expect the same will happen to us?

We all—Christians and sinners, old and young, rich and poor, educated and uneducated—go through valleys many times during our lives. Desperate circumstances like divorce or death can create valleys—or embarrassing ones like our kids getting lice, or inconvenient ones like a nosy neighbor or leaky faucet, or stressful ones like job or relationship issues—but each valley refines us. We should understand three things about valleys: they're accomplishing a work in us, we're already victorious through Christ, and we're not alone. John 16:33 says, *"These things I have spoken unto you, that in Me ye might have peace. In the world ye shall have tribulation: but be of good cheer; I have overcome the world."* When Jesus came to the earth and died as a man, He paid for whatever came along for us. He overcame the world. Though we will mature in every gate we pass through, the work doesn't stop. God will always be refining us. Now, He's beginning to test our mettle.

GOOD NEWS

Paradoxically, in our Christian journey valleys are good news. James 1:2-3 says, *"My brethren, count it all joy when ye fall into divers temptations; knowing this, that the trying of your faith worketh patience."* Here, in this Valley Gate, God can accomplish many things in us: patience, temperance, faith, righteousness. I once read a story about a mountain with trees on both sides. One side was sheltered, and the other wasn't. Because of the difference in exposure to severe weather, trees on the sheltered side had a much shorter life expectancy than those exposed to harsher weather. The same is true for us. Adversities create toughness in us to withstand whatever comes along. Valleys refine us. Romans 5:3-5 says, *"We glory in tribulations also: knowing that tribulation worketh patience; and patience, experience; and experience, hope: and hope maketh not ashamed...."* Each trial purifies us so we can become the man or woman God created us to be.

My aging mother sold her house in Arizona and moved closer to one of her children: me. I hadn't lived around her since I'd been an adult, so this was an adjustment for me. At first, having the extra responsibility of my mother threw a lot onto my already full plate with job, daughters in college, pastoral duties, and home tasks. Then, when she got ill, I found myself needing to come up with more hours than the day had. At times, I resented this until one day when I was really discouraged, and the Lord spoke to me. He said everything I did for my mother was to be done with gladness. In other words, I didn't *have* to do it; I *got* to do it. That revelation changed my attitude, and since then I've looked at many laborious things with a more positive attitude than I did in the past. God used that deep, deep valley of my mother's illness then death to teach me a lesson in finding wealth in the midst of the valleys.

FERTILITY

It would be nice to dwell on the mountain where feel-good experiences are constant, but we need to go to the valley to experience the reality of what God has for us and others. We all love those mountaintop experiences, but productivity usually happens while we're in the valley. When we're there, we turn more to God than when we're on the mountain. Each time we lean on Him, our greater dependency creates more maturity. Valleys are a place of enlarging our borders; mountains don't produce much growth because their land isn't as fertile as the valley.

Therefore, the first reason a Christian needs to go through the Valley Gate is that it provides fertility.[2] Even though we arrive there through troubles, we can find *"a good land...of brooks of water, of fountains and depths that spring out of valleys and hills"* and feed our troubled souls (Deut. 8:7). We can grow in valleys because greater fertility produces more fruit in our lives. Rich, fertile soil good for farming abounds in the valley. Though we taste the bitterness of the testing, *"the clods of the valley shall be sweet unto"* us because they produce whatever God desires in us (Job 21:33a). Here we can also sip sweetness of the waters, for *"He sendeth the springs into the valleys"* (Ps. 104:10a). How tasty and wondrous is that water that flows from the mountains into the low places of our lives.

BATTLE

The second thing that occurs in the valley is battle.[3] If we never fight battles, we can't achieve victories. Many biblical battles occur in valleys because it's easier to fight there than on a hill or mountain. The first biblical reference to battles occurs in the Valley of Siddim. In Genesis 14, Lot was taken prisoner by heathen kings; this abduction necessitated a rescue by Abraham. Though battles are always hard, this one turned into a God encounter. Abraham met Melchizedek, a king and priest—and thus an archetype of Jesus. Abraham honored him, paid tithes to him, and even shared wine and bread as a type of communion. Without his valley experience, Abraham would not have met this precursor of Jesus. Often, when we look back at our valley experiences, we find important things have occurred as a result of our own battle time. Battles make faith grow because we must believe God will create an outcome for our good, and *"all things work together for good to them that love God, to them who are the called according to His purpose"* (Rom. 8:28). We're called and headed to the Assignment Gate, so these things—even though at the time we can't see it—are working toward that assignment.

Sometimes battles not only teach us, but also magnify God; in them, His might is shown. Joshua battled against the Amorites in the Valley of Ajalon. This battle allowed God to be exalted throughout all time because the sun stood still for about a day so Joshua could achieve a victory (see Josh. 10:12-14). People of other cultures such as Egyptians, Chinese, Aztecs, Babylonians, and Mexicans have recorded in their history that time stood still for about one day. Astronomers' calculations with various calendars found a missing day that correlates with this battle.[4] Because God created the Earth, He surely knows how to slow rotations and revolutions to give His people a military advantage and Himself deserved glory.

Another event promoted Jesus when Lazarus died, a valley experience that made Jesus cry (see John 11). As hard as this valley was for Him and Lazarus' sisters, when Lazarus was raised from the dead, Jesus was exalted. When Jesus returned to Bethany, a great crowd came because *"much people of the Jews...knew...and they came not for Jesus' sake only, but that they might see Lazarus also, whom He had raised from the dead"* (John 12:9). Lazarus had become somewhat famous after his resurrection, so people were coming out in droves to see him as well as Jesus. This loss offered Jesus an opportunity to reach more souls. The valleys of Joshua and Jesus allowed God to demonstrate His sovereignty and might.

With battles, we assume there will be death. During the battle in the Valley Gate, we experience death to ourselves and whatever stands between us and God. Dying to the old man during battles is part of what it takes to create the man or woman God designed. Psalm 23:4 tells us that no matter what happens in our valley, we must not be afraid, for the Lord not only is taking care of us but also is preparing us for what is to come. Romans 8:17-18 says,

And if children...of God, and joint-heirs with Christ; if so be that we suffer with Him, that we may be also glorified together. For...the sufferings of this present time are not worthy to be compared with the glory which shall be revealed in us.

Battles prepare us for that glory time.

JUDGMENT

Another advantage of valleys is judgment.[5] Here, God judges our actions to prepare us for our ultimate goal. Remember, the purpose of our walk with the Lord is to get into the Assignment Gate and reach our destiny. Often we're unable to do that because in the valley we lose focus and become preoccupied with problems instead of solutions. Judgment in the valley happens so we get rid of the idols we cling to. In the Kidron Valley, Josiah destroyed things, places, and people worshipping Baal and Asherah to rebuild devotion to God (see 2 Kings 23). In the Kishon Valley, Elijah killed Baal's prophets (see 1 Kings 18). We nurse our own idols—hurt, bitterness, rejection—when God wants us to destroy them. Judgment comes in many ways, but it gets us back on the right path and shows us what we're made of.

We stand in danger of His judgment here if we refuse to let Him do His work in us. In the entrance to the Valley Gate, shards of pottery that were broken, discarded, and unusable were thrown out. When a potter creates something, he has in mind what he wants that piece to be—a vase, a mug, a plate. Bringing the clay into its destiny, however, is a process. The potter prepares it before he can even begin to mold it. He kneads it thoroughly to get out air bubbles and small impurities embedded in the clay. If he doesn't remove uncleanness, when the time comes to fire the piece, it won't withstand the kiln's heat, which proves whether it's solid and useful. If impurities remain, they'll show up during the firing process, and the vessel will likely crack. Then it can't be used because those things that affect its worth are still there. The same goes for us.

This time when God is removing our foibles can be uncomfortable; sometimes it just plain hurts. But the kneading process makes us pliable and brings us into alignment with His plan. Impurities that remain in us may be hidden to others or even ourselves, but if we don't allow God to remove these issues, He simply can't use us. As long as we're eager for the Potter's will, hope still exists. Jeremiah 18:4 says, *"The vessel that he made of clay was marred in the hand of the potter: so he made it again another vessel, as seemed good to the potter to make it."* Though at times we're like broken pottery, we must put ourselves again into the Potter's hands to allow Him to do with us as He pleases. If we fail and don't get back up, we can become the unusable, discarded pottery by the gate. If we let the Potter make and remake us His way, though, we have a great chance for success. The prophet said, *"I will pour down the stones thereof into the valley, and I will discover the foundations thereof"* (Mic. 1:6b). What are the foundations He will discover in us during our time of judgment fire?

RENEWED FERTILITY

In addition to the fertility, battles, and judgment we experience in the valley, for some, time spent here can ultimately bring a renewed fertility as the Potter remakes the vessel.[6] Just as David traveled from the *"shadow of death"* to *"green pastures"* (Ps. 23:2,4), a trip to the valley also allows dried springs to flow again. In Genesis, we read that Abraham dug wells that later were stopped up by the Philistines. Then,

> *Isaac digged again the wells of water, which they had digged in the days of Abraham his father....And Isaac's servants digged in the valley, and found there a well of springing water* (Genesis 26:18-19).

Often wells of productivity seem to be destroyed by satan and no longer flowing. We may have fallen and now feel we can't be victorious, but the valley brings us the fertility we had before, and even more. Proverbs 6:31 says if a thief is caught, he must return sevenfold. We know he's always trying to steal, kill, and destroy, but valleys enable us to find strength to continue on to renewed fertility.

My sister is a wonderful example of renewed fertility. As a young woman, she was beautiful, musically gifted, God-oriented, and college educated. In essence, she had the world at her fingertips. She married well, had a family, moved into the house of anyone's dreams—and lost her desire to put God first. The fertility of her life dried up with the revelation of her husband's infidelity and their subsequent divorce. She was emotionally and spiritually beaten up and beaten down until God stepped in and wooed her back into fellowship with Him. He led her to move out of state, get a PhD, and ultimately work for a Christian organization. She is now a Christian author with many published books and loves God with all her heart. That's renewed fertility.

The valley brings back good to us in spite of what our lives were before. Hosea 2:15a says, *"I will give her her vineyards from thence, and the valley of Achor for a door of hope."* In the Valley of Achor, Achan and his family were killed after he took forbidden items from Jericho that God had instructed be destroyed (see Josh. 7). Now, though, from *Achor,* which means "trouble," hope can spring.[7] That's renewed fertility. Isaiah 65:10 says, *"Sharon shall be a fold of flocks, and the valley of Achor a place for the herds to lie down in."* God's promising that, from trouble and disaster, Achor will ultimately become a peaceful *"place for the herds to lie down."* That's renewed fertility. Isaiah 40:4a says, *"Every valley shall be exalted, and every mountain and hill shall be made low."* So, what was bad will now be changed to good. Isaiah 41:18 and Luke 3:5 tell us God will make rivers and fountains in the valley and let springs come into dry lands. So, in our low places, we'll find our thirst quenched by rivers and fountains He opens in valleys. That's renewed fertility.

SAMSON

Samson's life demonstrates all these aspects of valleys. He traveled through a valley when his father-in-law gave his wife to another man (see Judg. 15:2). As a result, he went into the battle phase in Judges 15, caught 300 foxes, tied torches to their tails, and burned the Philistines' fields. Then, he slew 1,000 Philistines with the jawbone of an ass, and in Lehi, God made water to drink from the same jawbone. Through Samson's exploits, God used the battle to demonstrate His might. In addition, he showed great fertility. In Judges 16:2, he had some valley time as he was surrounded and faced certain death by the hands of the Gazites. To escape, he carried a 4,000-pound gate and posts from Gaza to Hebron, about 20-30 miles away in the hills.[8] That's fertility. Then Samson experienced judgment. In Gaza, he was betrayed by Delilah, who was from the Valley of Sorek, which means "hissing," and was blinded.[9] Doesn't that describe satan perfectly—the hissing snake that tempts and then brings blindness to those tricked by it? Judgment came when Samson followed the heathen and lost both his sight and freedom.

However, God had renewed fertility for him. While he was in prison, his hair began to grow. When he was led to a banquet to amuse the Philistines, he grabbed pillars and killed the entire group. His victory in death created a slaughter of 3,000 Philistines, more killed than at any other time in his life. Just as Samson's valley life ran the gamut of what valleys can produce, our lives do, too, at certain times. Maybe the job we lost gave us time to write that book we've always wanted to write. Maybe God used our child's arrest to inspire us to begin a jail ministry. Maybe we fail in a protracted battle to keep from losing our house, but God uses that loss to give us something better or to remove ties to this city so we can go to another, the place of our destiny.

Maybe we've sunk as low as we can in a life of addiction. That doesn't mean He's finished with us. In an instant, God can turn us around and employ those experiences for our later ministry. Plenty of preachers have used past blunders—drugs, satan worshiping, illegal activities—as a later testimony in their ministries about a God who brings renewed fertility. Through all these adversities, our character is also being refined. From patience to kindness to trust in the Father, God can take devastating events and make us into what He wants us to be. We must celebrate rather than groan because of what's happening to us. He has a plan, and valleys help accomplish that plan.

CONCLUSION

What God does for us in the valley is more than we can measure. When my daughters were born, we three began a journey. When they were four and we became a single-parent family, we went through many valleys—from broken bones to broken hearts—but each of those valleys did a work in my children. Maybe the problem brought forth patience, obedience, problem-solving skills, encouragement, or other things—but each trial had a part in the women they ultimately became. Through all of our issues, they learned one thing: they could count on Mom for everything from helping them prepare for a test to holding their hands when they were nervous. They learned to trust and love me even more with each valley from infancy into adulthood.

That's what we also learn in our spiritual valleys. As we travel our roads and hit the valleys, we begin to understand that our Father is doing a work in "growing us up right" with a character that makes Him a proud Abba. While we're maturing, He is teaching us a deeper love and confidence in Him. Wherever we're walking, mountain or valley, we rest assured that He's there for us, no matter what.

Valleys are demanding but provide natural and spiritual growth, for they're more fertile than mountains. We learn much from our trials. As hurtful as those experiences can be, they change us and our walk with God. Valleys refine us to produce the fruit He wants: *"love, joy, peace, longsuffering, gentleness, goodness, faith, meekness, temperance"* (Gal. 5:22-23). He has a work to do in us, and through high and low places we learn complete dependence on His ability to care for us. This is a low point in our Christian life and can fill us with emotions that make us question our trip, not only in the valley but also with God. Our time here, however, often depends on our attitude and how well we learn to rely on Him. Valleys bring humility, let us grow to be like Jesus, and teach that God is with us at all times. Hardships refine us: *"Before I was afflicted I went astray: but now have I kept Thy word"* (Ps. 119:67). Sounds like a lesson we began learning at the Sheep Gate.

CHAPTER

5

THE DUNG (REFUSE) GATE: REFINING OUR CHARACTER

But the dung gate repaired Malchiah the son of Rechab, the ruler of part of Bethhaccerem; he built it, and set up the doors thereof, the locks thereof, and the bars thereof (Nehemiah 3:14).

When I was young, my family went to church incessantly—Wednesday night youth group, Saturday night, Sunday morning broadcast, Sunday school, and Sunday night church. If we had revival, we went every night. That was our family's entire social life; Jesus was what our whole existence was built around. When someone spends that much time with a church family, everyone knows each other intimately. At our church, all of us young people became friends and understood each other's foibles.

One family had several children older than I. Most weekends when we went to church, people would tell us that these children had backslidden that week. Inevitably, one of them would go to the altar and get resaved each Sunday. Even as a child, I knew something was wrong with that picture. If salvation is so fragile that it can't withstand mistakes that come with everyday living, then the simple plan Jesus died for is not as perfect as we think. Some people don't understand that within the progression of the gates, God makes allowances for our "screw-ups." I've had plenty of those, and He didn't tell me I needed to become His child all over again. Then again, His plan was never for us to be born again and then stop growing. That evolution is constant and forever.

Salvation is a process many people don't understand. That word means wholeness in body, spirit, and soul. First, the spirit is justified (salvation). Then, the mind has ongoing sanctification (renewing of the mind). Finally, the body is moving toward glorification, which will be accomplished completely in the resurrection. Although our spirit is saved, our minds and bodies go through a continual process of salvation, and sanctification is an important part. When we stumble in our quest to grow, God doesn't give up on us. With sanctification, we understand that God doesn't approve of some stinking things in us, but He still loves us—His children—and wants us to get better. That's where the Dung Gate comes in.

THE DUNG GATE

Since the map (see Appendix 1) shows that the Valley Gate is quite a distance from the Dung Gate, we could surmise that we've all spent a good while there. Maybe we even went through it twice, as Nehemiah did. However, just when we finish the Valley Gate and think things are going to be easier, along comes the Dung Gate. In previous gates, the Lord used adversities, an unfolding love for the Shepherd, and an increasing knowledge of Him to create new character in us. At this point, another transformation takes place: we get rid of a large portion of remaining undesirable traits. The Valley Gate began to change whatever stood between us and God while we relied on His wisdom in the trials. Now, God shows what's still in our character that He wants gone. As we move toward our divine assignment, He must get rid of whatever will hinder us, *"For whom the Lord loveth He chasteneth, and scourgeth every son whom He receiveth"* (Heb. 12:6). He does all this disciplining for the same reason we chasten our own kids: He loves us. We all must pass through this gate, for even Jesus came in through the dung gate of the manger.

The gate was repaired by *Malchijah* (the Lord my king, my counselor), son of *Rechab* (square, chariot with team of four horses).[1] These names are significant because at this gate, we take a more profound stand to make Jesus King of our lives. As we get rid of undesirable things, we become a more solid Christian. Jerusalem citizens took their trash through this gate to the garbage pit, *Gehenna*, to be burned.[2] *Gehenna* is a Latin word that Hebrews later associated with the wickeds' judgment by fire.[3] Garbage in us should also go through this gate to be destroyed by God's fire. That dump burned constantly, just as purging the things that are offensive to God is an ongoing process. When one is gone, another becomes apparent so we can work on it. Filth must be removed to allow God's purposes to emerge.

A USEFUL TOOL

Dung was viewed differently from other waste in Bible times and didn't get burned in *Gehenna*. Animal dung was regarded as functional, not dirty (see Ezek. 4:15). It was piled around the outside of the wall to be used as fertilizer or made into blocks to burn for heating or cooking. That usefulness is good news for us. Unlike my childhood friends who believed mistakes separated them from the Father, each mistake actually can play a part in what God ultimately makes us into. The wonderful thing about the Dung Gate is that the Lord weaves former errors into the new fabric He creates for us. I know people who have endured divorce, drug abuse, alcoholism, abortion, or other previous mistakes—and God used these as ministering points to others. God can utilize anything, even dung, to accomplish His will.

Religion often gets this gate out of order. Many well-meaning Christians try to counsel new converts to purge their lives as soon as they come to the Lord. The truth is, this is a continuing process in a Christian's life; if we thought we had to clean up everything when we first got saved, we'd be too overwhelmed and give up. Many have gone that route.

When my parents were pastoring, a young couple came to church and accepted Christ. They were excited and on fire for God, so they entered the Fish Gate and told everyone about God. They brought many to church who were born again as a result. However, the couple didn't dress the way more established Christians did. A well-intentioned but misdirected person took it upon himself to tell them they should appear more "godly." It so discouraged the couple that they quit going to church altogether, and as far as I know never did again. In contrast, other new sheep whose older Christian brothers and sisters let God do the cleaning, grew up and changed in God's time. As more mature Christians, we must understand this as our new brothers and sisters begin their own gates journey. God knows how to modify them His way without devastating them. We shouldn't fret about changing until we're mature enough in Him that this process is a natural extension of our growth.

A NATURAL PROGRESSION

One day I was making one of my favorite holiday items: fudge. I had all my ingredients and turned my saucepan on just the right temperature. I'd left my glasses upstairs but figured I'd made it often enough I'd do fine even though I couldn't see the recipe too well. Then the phone rang. I was talking and adding things to the mix when suddenly the melted concoction looked strange. I finally broke down, got my glasses, and hung up the phone to devote my attention to what I was doing. Because of my inattention, I had put the milk in at the wrong time, and it had become hard with a strange texture. I tried to salvage the mess, but when it cooled, it tasted terrible. When my girls came in, they oohed and aahed about the plate of fudge on the counter until they tasted it. I'd come up with a product that looked like fudge, but because I'd gotten things out of order, it hadn't come into the full potential of fudge. Even their friend Chase, a teenaged garbage disposal, wouldn't eat it after the first bite. Similarly, when we get out of order in our Christian journey, we can seem to be OK, but we won't grow up to our potential unless we go through the recipe God has prepared for us.

Because our experiences have challenged us to get to know God, many things dropped off naturally in the first gates. We changed because our "want to's" changed. Now's the time for us to look seriously at what God asks us to get rid of. Second Corinthians 7:1 says,

Having therefore these promises, dearly beloved, let us cleanse ourselves from all filthiness of the flesh and spirit, perfecting holiness in the fear of God.

That's what happens here. This gate brings us closer to God while it scours us from stinking dung: lust, lack of integrity, greed, hurt, bitterness, pride, laziness, jealousy, hatred, insecurity, gluttony, selfishness, gossip, envy, lying, fear, anger, being overly critical, rebellion, unforgiveness, stubbornness—get the picture? Most of that list hits each of us, and we can probably think of more. To grow, we must throw out sins as we did in the valley but now on a larger scale. Solomon told us that *"where no oxen are, the crib is clean: but much increase is by the strength of the ox"* (Prov. 14:4). In essence, he's saying that if we're going to accomplish anything in God's Kingdom, we must understand that dung is in ourselves and others, and dung makes messes.

The first biblical reference to dung was associated with sacrifice, and God began to deal with us about sacrificing ourselves way back in the Sheep Gate. In Exodus 29:14, Leviticus 4:11, and Numbers 19:5, His people were ordered to present total sacrifices: the animal, its flesh, and its dung as a sin offering. Today, God still wants us to give everything as *"a living sacrifice, holy, acceptable"* to Him (Rom. 12:1). We became new when we sacrificed our lives at the start of this journey. Now, we must present ourselves wholly as sacrifices, including the stinking dung of our lives. Hebrews 12:1b says, *"Let us lay aside every weight, and the sin which doth so easily beset us, and let us run with patience the race that is set before us."* We're in this pursuit to find our purpose and be used in that calling. That dung, the imperfections in the Potter's vessel, must be removed before that final firing process.

WHAT DEFINES SIN?

God loves us, but He doesn't wink at sin. We must keep in mind that He *"hath not called us unto uncleanness, but unto holiness"* (1 Thess. 4:7). Just as some people badger new converts to become too perfect too soon, some don't teach them we're to break free from the world and seek sanctification. A recent trend in some churches is to seek converts without offending anyone with teachings about righteousness. Though this produces many church attendees, it doesn't show the importance of gates where, by God's design, character is refined. When we wallow in sin, that dung creates a stench to God, so we must *"lay aside"* weights of sin and be the godly men and women He desires us to be. Exodus 30:23-25 gives ingredients for anointing oil; one of those is 500 shekels of *cassia,* a laxative used for purging. If we're to be anointed vessels for God, He wants us to seek His will for what should be purged from us.

What defines sin? That answer is as varied as the people who commit their lives to the Lord. Paul says to *"work out your own salvation with fear and trembling. For it is God which worketh in you both to will and to do of His good pleasure"* (Phil. 2:12-13). To me, that Scripture says it's up to you and God to find His will for you. God is the one we should seek to please, and He celebrates differences. Snowflakes, soil types, DNA, fingerprints, voice patterns, hair follicles—even the irises in our eyes are all different. About 1 million types of animals live on this planet: 8,600 varieties of birds;[4] over 21,000 species of fish;[5] 800,000 varieties of insects; and, according to estimates, 1 million to 10 million more that are not yet discovered.[6] God understands we're different; He created us and the whole planet that way.

By extension, then, neither does one size fit all in our salvation. For example, some Christians believe cutting hair, wearing pants, dancing, or using makeup is wrong. Others don't see a problem with those things, but have issues with wearing jewelry. Someone thinks drinking is wrong while another thinks drinking a glass of wine with his meal is OK. I know people who won't eat pork products while others won't eat Chinese food. Good, devoted Christians believe in things far across the spectrum from one another, but all are sold out to the Lord. Some of us are made to be apple trees and some to be pear trees. Some are short while some are tall. We're different in every way because He created us to be. Our character also has been crafted by God, and it's He who determines how to best refine it.

LIBERTY

Often, we become too hung up on rules. If we're overly rigid, we forget about the law of love Christ brought. Then, when we have to work so hard to observe the law without the freedom of love, it becomes a bondage to us. Jesus didn't die for us to be bound to anything but

God. Galatians 5:1 says, *"Stand fast therefore in the liberty wherewith Christ hath made us free, and be not be entangled again with the yoke of bondage."* He bought our freedom even from the rules religion imposes and which can become rotten like dung, too. The law shouldn't be a battering ram but rather a shaping tool to love and help those whom God cherishes. That doesn't mean, however, that anything goes. On the contrary, God has high standards by which we should live. Many Christians try to go as far as possible toward sin and still be OK with God. The Dung Gate tells us we should be as close as possible to Him because we love and want to please Him.

Unfortunately, some take this liberty to work out their own salvation as an excuse to do anything, knowing God will forgive. Paul tells us that liberty from the law is not a license to sin: *"Shall we continue in sin, that grace may abound? God forbid. How shall we, that are dead to sin, live any longer therein?"* (Rom. 6:1b-2). He's asking, "Do we willfully sin because Jesus paid the price?" Paul says, "No way, José!" We live with a higher standard than the law gave us—love. Love says we're to live for others without being people pleasers. We're to live to please God, and putting others above our own desires pleases Him. Galatians 5:14 says, *"For all the law is fulfilled in one word, even in this; Thou shalt love thy neighbour as thyself."* This type of love is *agape*, the kind with which Jesus loved both God and man. It's the love that says, "Though I'd like to do this, I love You enough, God, to forgo my desires for Your Kingdom." We began developing that kind of love as sheep for the Shepherd, and now we're listening to the sound of His voice and following whatever He says because of our love for Him.

So though we operate in liberty, as we get closer to God, we should consider our choices more diligently and walk in integrity. I remember a minister who would pray for people to be delivered from cigarettes, then go to his car and smoke. Though many good Christians haven't been able to give up cigarettes, saying one thing and doing another was wrong. Weaker brothers watch us for their cues about how to live. Romans 14:1-3 reminds us that some of us possess a little and some a lot of faith, so we must be careful that we don't cause another to fall while we're exercising our liberty in the Lord. For example, I love the taste of Bloody Mary mix. I don't drink alcohol in it because that's my conviction, but when I buy it or put it in my refrigerator, I may cause someone else to lose confidence in me as she looks to my actions as an older Christian and godly example. Sometimes, God requires us to do what others believe, not because our choices are wrong, but because we don't want to discourage one who's weaker.

I once knew a couple who got saved but didn't believe drinking was wrong. They were on fire and operated prolifically in the Fish Gate, trying to win others into the Kingdom. She worked at a restaurant, and they spread the message of Jesus to whoever would listen. A few weeks later, they decided to drink at that restaurant. While they sat at a corner table, I heard several customers around me comment they thought the couple had gotten saved and wondered why they were drinking. Now, I'm not judging whether drinking is right or wrong. That's between you and God. However, that night, much of the good that had been done by their excitement about the Lord was undone by their actions. We all must be careful that our *"good* [not] *be evil spoken of"* (Rom. 14:16), for we're emissaries of God to the world. We must seek His will, and His desire is for us to obey Him, no matter what He asks us to do.

SIN

In my opinion, if we're born again, we'll go to Heaven even though we hold onto some of our faults. However, ending up in Heaven isn't our only goal; we may never be given an opportunity to fulfill our ministry here if dung remains in us. Everything we struggle with is correctable with God's help. Often works of the flesh, however, become so ingrained in us we no longer desire or see the need to get rid of them. They've become part of our character and show our lack of integrity. First Timothy 4:2 says some speak *"lies in hypocrisy; having their conscience seared with a hot iron."* They're no longer attempting to do what God requires and feel no remorse for their sin. Those are the broken shards of pottery that can't be used anymore. We need to be careful sins don't become part of our character, get embedded within us, and proceed out of our hearts (see Matt. 15:18). With willful sin, we risk losing what we gained in the Sheep Gate.

For if we sin willfully after that we have received the knowledge of the truth, there remaineth no more sacrifice for sins, but a certain fearful looking for of judgment and fiery indignation, which shall devour the adversaries (Hebrews 10:26-27).

We all possess inherent negative qualities because we're flesh and blood, so we all must pass through the Dung Gate. Romans 3:23 says, *"All have sinned, and come short of the glory of God"*—you, me, your pastor, your mother, the Pope, everyone. You may have the "biggies" taken care of, but what about other sins distancing you from God? Galatians 5:19-21, Second Corinthians 12:20, and Colossians 3:5,8-9 list sins ranging from adultery to envy; all can keep us from taking our place in God's work—but He's interested in cleaning up our hearts. Solomon says to *"keep thy heart with all diligence; for out of it are the issues of life....Let thine eyes look right on.... Ponder the path of thy feet... remove thy foot from evil"* (Prov. 4:23-27). The road we travel to God's Kingdom is straight. Whether we want just to find Heaven or fulfill our destiny here on Earth, pleasing Him must be our only goal.

CONCLUSION

When my daughter was a junior high teenager, she got into trouble with me for some mischief she and her friend had done at a neighborhood video store. One morning we were getting ready for school in our usual chaotic fashion. The blow dryer was blaring, and the *TODAY* Show was droning in the background. That day, she followed me from room to room and fussed with me that my punishing her for what she'd done at the video store was unfair. Then she said something she thought would be a perfect argument.

She jutted her jaw out, put her hands on her hips, and blurted in her crisp, snide voice, "It's not fair. Mandy didn't get in trouble at all. Her mom doesn't care what she does."

I stopped brushing my teeth and turned to face her. She continued to stare defiantly at me for a few seconds. "Jennifer, for as long as you live, I hope you never say that about me." She stood there for a moment, then walked away. The subject was never brought up again.

God is our caring, loving parent; thus, He sometimes has to do things to impact our characters. Maybe He's looking toward our Assignment Gate. Maybe He sees danger in our future. Maybe He wants us to be more caring or loving. Maybe He sees that something in us will hurt our success in life. Whatever the reason, He desires to change us simply because He loves us and wants us to mature just as I wanted Jennifer to learn a lesson about respect and consideration for others that would follow her into adulthood.

Some Christians stop their journey in the Dung Gate because there's too much they don't want to give up. Paul, who relinquished everything that was his old life, was persecuted and tempted in every way, yet he said,

> *...I count all things but loss for the excellency of the knowledge of Christ Jesus my Lord: for whom I have suffered the loss of all things, and do count them but dung, that I may win Christ* (Philippians 3:8).

Sin is merely for a season; we're working on the eternal. What we gain far outweighs our sacrifice. The Dung Gate is unpleasant but necessary, and God stays with us during this whole process.

Yesterday it was wonderful manna; today it is dung. We can't live on what was new yesterday. We must seek fresh nutrition to replace it each day and find what God wants now. He desires for us to get better and rewards our efforts. I love Psalm 18:24, which says, *"Therefore hath the Lord recompensed me according to my righteousness, according to the cleanness of my hands in His eyesight."* Nothing we can do earns the salvation we found in the Sheep Gate, but our rewards come by the cleanliness of our lives. Nearly everything we ever do that matters is difficult—college, marriage, child rearing, employment.

This gate has been hard, too; but after this, a change happens. The wall begins to move upward as we go toward the Fountain Gate. Our focus starts to change, too. Before, we were more concerned about ourselves and how our walk impacted us. Now, we're traveling toward God's glory.

CHAPTER

6

THE FOUNTAIN GATE: GETTING FILLED

Then I went on to the gate of the fountain, and to the king's pool: but there was no place for the beast that was under me to pass (Nehemiah 2:14).

But the gate of the fountain repaired Shallun the son of Colhozeh, the ruler of part of Mizpah; he built it, and covered it, and set up the doors thereof, the locks thereof, and the bars thereof, and the wall of the pool of Siloah by the king's garden, and unto the stairs that go down from the city of David (Nehemiah 3:15).

When I was a little girl growing up in Ohio, I loved to go to Indiana and visit my many aunts' and cousins' houses. My favorite place was Aunt Cleo's, despite the fact that we planted a garden there and had to work it on the weekends. Down the graveled road a ways from her house, a creek rippled across fossiled rocks. Horses often populated the stalls or grazed in the less-than-pristine arena. My female cousins, older and thus objects of my adoration, were cheerleaders and beautiful. Their brothers played with us like they enjoyed having us kids there. Aunt Cleo was not like most of our other paternal aunts: she actually knew our names and didn't just refer to us as one of Ernie's many children. She always had plenty of goodies cooked up and seemed to delight in having us around.

Her large yard and gray-shingled house had lots to explore, including an outhouse there by necessity and a ramshackle barn that had seen better days but gave plenty of inspiration for getting into mischief. My favorite thing on the whole property, however, was in the corner of the yard: a rusty, metal pump with a banged-up, ancient, aluminum ladle hung on a wire. It took a while to get the mechanics, but eventually, I could pump fresh, cold water from the well beneath the concrete base. Unlike water in other places, that drink was so refreshing I can still remember it today. Holy Spirit is like that cool freshness. If at this point in our Christian growth we choose to be baptized in Holy Spirit, we'll find a refreshing drink that will serve us as long as we live. God knows us personally, not just as one of His billions of creations on this planet. He delights in us. He knows our names and situations. And He understands how Holy Spirit will fit into the plan for our lives.

FILLED WITH THE SPIRIT

After the Valley and Dung Gates where debris was cleaned from us, Holy Spirit now brings a refreshing like water from a deep, cool, country well. Water is often linked to Holy Spirit, many times through baptism. Jesus was filled with Holy Spirit while He was in the water (see Luke 3:22). That metaphor of water baptism is taken a step further when John says though he was baptizing with water, the Messiah would be *"he which baptizeth with the Holy Ghost"* (John 1:33c). After He was risen, Jesus confirmed that analogy to the disciples; He said that they would *"be baptized with the Holy Ghost not many days hence"* (Acts 1:5b). Although being baptized with water generally accompanies salvation, this baptism of fire, Holy Spirit, is in addition to what we received when we were first saved.

Varying opinions exist about when we receive Holy Spirit, but I believe He's part of our salvation, and when we're saved *"by one Spirit are we all baptized into one body"* (1 Cor. 12:13a). In others words, when we become a member of the Body of Christ, part of the package is Holy Spirit, a gift, we just need to receive (see Luke 11:13). Peter told the sinners at Pentecost to *"repent, and be baptized every one of you in the name of Jesus Christ for the remission of sins, and ye shall receive the gift of the Holy Ghost"* (Acts 2:38). In Nehemiah 2:14, his animal had no room to pass through this gate. A donkey symbolizes human effort, and entering into a Holy Spirit walk is not achieved by human exertion. As Solomon's temple was built, the sound of hammers couldn't be heard because it indicated human effort. Priests could not wear wool mixed with linen because it could cause sweating, which meant man's toil. Holy Spirit is a gift, so we just have to receive and allow Him to do His work in us. However, there's a difference between the *gift* and the *gifts* of Holy Spirit, which are His manifestations.

At this gate is when we become filled with Him, or Spirit-filled, and He begins to move on and through us. Though in First Corinthians Paul said we are *"all baptized into one body,"* he says we also should *"be filled with the Spirit"* (Eph. 5:18b). He's making that distinction because there's a difference in the levels of where we can be with Holy Spirit. Saul went through the process of conversion when he believed in Jesus and said, *"Lord, what wilt thou have me to do?"* (Acts 9:6). Later Ananias called him *"Brother Saul"* (Acts 9:17). However, he was baptized in Holy Spirit several days later (see Acts 9:18). Generally, there's a time that passes between salvation and baptism of Holy Spirit.

That doesn't mean, though, some people don't go through this gate earlier. Several people in the Bible were Spirit-filled even before Jesus: Elizabeth was filled with Holy Spirit when she heard Mary's voice (see Luke 1:41); Zacharias was filled at John's circumcision (see Luke 1:67); Simeon operated in revelations of Holy Spirit (see Luke 2:25-26); and John received an infilling of Holy Spirit in his mother's womb (see Luke 1:15). When we pastored, a little girl who attended our church was already knowledgeable in the deep things of God, including travail and right-on dreams. Other times, I've seen people become filled with Holy Spirit as they got saved and spoke in tongues right there. Those were the ones who wanted something more from the beginning, so as they were learning to become sheep, they also began mastering the gifts God had given for an overcoming lifestyle. I became filled with Holy Spirit when I was just a child and learned to operate in the gifts at an early age, too. But even though some get deeper into Holy Spirit faster than usual, the earlier gates are still crucial to bring us to an understanding that leads to the maturity required.

THE FOUNTAIN GATE

Most Christians, however, haven't yet come into this Holy Spirit walk, which requires abandonment. They have many reasons for not pressing in—it's weird, their church doesn't condone it, it seems unnecessary, it's deeper than they've really wanted to go. This is a point where we can grow exponentially, so we make a conscious decision to become *filled* with Him and take advantage of *everything* He has to offer. When Paul said in Ephesians 5:18 to *"be filled with the Spirit,"* that word is the Greek *pleroo, meaning "(be, make) full."*[1] It carrries the implication that it "does not stop with a single experience but is maintained by continually being filled."[2] This is where Holy Spirit becomes our life, *zoe*, which allows us to live above circumstances. When our own children are growing, we give them many things that will provide an advantage in their lives—an education, maybe a car, or help with a down payment on a house. We realize life can be challenging, so out of love we give them something that will be a boon to them. That's what our Father does for us with Holy Spirit, who gives strength, power, and knowledge to make our journey more successful. He's like our big brother who not only always looks out for us in situations, but also warns us; He provides us with weapons; He comforts, guides, and does many, many other things. Holy Spirit has consummate ability and allows us to enter into God's rest to do His work through us.

The gate was rebuilt by *Shallun,* which means "perfect; agreeable," the son of *Col-Hozeh* (every prophet), leader of the district of *Mizpah* (a watch tower).[3] Each of these definitions describes Holy Spirit—perfect, agreeable, a prophet, and a watch tower. At this gate we can go as deep as we want and find limitless tools our Father has placed at our disposal through Holy Spirit.

Throughout Scripture, Holy Spirit is represented by many things—a rushing mighty wind (see Acts 2:2), fire, rivers, water under pressure. Each description of Holy Spirit's representation has an element of extra power. As a matter of fact, in Acts 4:31, that power was demonstrated when as Peter finished his talk to the Sanhedrin, the place shook as people received Holy Spirit. This shaking creates amazing things. That power, like a soda when you open it after the shaking, comes in this gate like water under pressure—a fountain.

Not all Scriptures referring to Holy Spirit use the word *fountain*, though, because words relating to "water" are often interchangeable. For example, in Jeremiah 17:13 the word *fountain* is *maqowr*: "a source (of water...) fountain, issue, spring, well."[4] That same word is translated as *"spring"* in Proverbs 25:26, but in Proverbs 10:11 it's translated as a *"well."* Other Scriptures are also the same word but have different translations that relate to water sources. Therefore, when the biblical translation doesn't literally say, "fountain," the implication is often there since those water terms are used interchangeably.

When God told Moses to speak to the rock at Kadesh and instead he struck it, a fountain came forth (see Num. 20:2-13). I believe this was an analogy to Holy Spirit. In past times, Moses had done miracles other ways with his rod, but this time God wanted to accomplish His will a new way. David said God *"turned the rock into a standing water, the flint into a fountain of waters"* (Ps. 114:8). Jesus came to bring a new thing—Holy Spirit—a fresh fountain flowing forth from the rock. When He left, He made a place for Holy Spirit to be released on the Day of Pentecost (see Acts 2:2). Joel had prophesied about this time when he said God would *"pour out* [His] *spirit upon all flesh"* (Joel 2:28a). The Hebrew word for "pour" is *shaphak*, "to spill forth...gush out, pour (out), shed (out)."[5] When Acts 2:17 quotes this same Scripture, it uses an even stronger Greek word, *ekchuno*: "to pour forth, to bestow, gush (pour) out, run greedily (out), shed (abroad, forth), spill."[6] These two references to God's promise then fulfillment of Holy Spirit are described in terms of water gushing or running out "greedily"—a fountain.

LIVING WATER

John quoted Jesus who spoke of Holy Spirit in terms of a river, again a powerful designation of water. Whoever receives Holy Spirit, *"out of his belly shall flow rivers of living water. (But this spake He of the Spirit...)"* (John 7:38b-39). The translation of "river" is *potamos,* "a current, brook...flood, river, stream, water."[7] Holy Spirit now fills the belly that was filled with dung yesterday. This *"living water"* is a concept Scripture refers to often. In John 4:10-14, Jesus and the Samaritan woman discuss living water in context of that drink after which she'd never again thirst. John also says, the *"the Lamb...shall lead them unto living fountains [pege] of waters..."* (Rev. 7:17).[8] He uses the same word as *"a well [pege] of water springing up into everlasting life"* (John 4:14) and says God will give this fountain [pege] freely (see Rev. 21:6). Deuteronomy 8:7 says, *"God bringeth thee into a good land, a land of brooks of water, of fountains and depths that spring out of valleys and hills."* The Fountain Gate represents that fertile, watered land of Holy Spirit, Who fills whatever empty spots are in our lives and exerts quiet pressure to flow from within.

CHAY MAYIM

Holy Spirit is alive within our walls, and Jerusalem's fountain demonstrates this. Zechariah 13:1 says, *"There shall be a fountain opened to the house of David and to the inhabitants of Jerusalem for sin and for uncleanness."* This literally happens at the Fountain Gate, which gets its name because it's near the Pool of Siloam. Clean water comes from the east at the Spring of Gihon ("to burst forth") in the Kidron Valley.[9] If you check Appendix 1, water comes via Hezekiah's Tunnel into the Pool of Siloam, which then becomes fresh water, not stagnant. Like Gihon, Holy Spirit bursts forth, too, in our giftings and brings fresh revelation because it is fresh water carried into us through Jesus.

Throughout its history, Jerusalem had three tunnel systems—Warren's Shaft (before David), the Siloam Channel (at the beginning of the 2nd millennium B.C.), and Hezekiah's Tunnel (701 B.C.).[10] Hezekiah built the tunnel in the face of an impending Assyrian siege. He wanted to rechannel the Spring of Gihon into the Pool of Siloam so Jerusalem couldn't be cut off from its water supply (see 2 Chron. 32). In the late nineteenth century someone found inscriptions describing when and how the tunnel was built.[11] It winds around because builders progressed from two sides and met in the middle. This resembles our progress with God; we rarely sail smoothly from one point to another, but our trek is filled with zigs, zags, and uncertainties. Sometimes in our circuitous Christian journey, we might momentarily lose our way, and then Jesus meets us right there to take us to fresh water.

That water that flows from the Spring of Gihon into the Pool of Siloam was called *chay mayim*, Hebrew for "living water," a type of Holy Spirit.[12] *Chay* is the same word used when Adam named all living animals and when Noah took living animals into the ark. When we become Spirit-filled, Holy Spirit is a living Person Who takes up residence inside us. Jesus said *chay mayim* is available to us when He told the woman at the well He would give her *"living water"* (John 4:10). Holy Spirit's waters can empower us for whatever our Christian journey brings. When we enter this gate, we foster a deeper, more powerful walk with God and will never be the same.

In the Gospel of John, Jesus taught in the temple during the Feast of Tabernacles, a festivity memorializing Moses' wilderness trek, the ingathering of the harvest, and God's provision with water at Meribah (see Num. 20:2-13). The celebration incorporated seven days of the priests drawing water from the Pool of Siloam, carrying it in a golden pitcher to the temple, and then pouring it on the altar. This ritual represented how God provided a way in the wilderness every day to quench His people's thirst, but each day, like manna, water had to be replenished. Jesus used this event to show the limitations of what the priests had to offer when,

> [On] *the last day...of the feast, Jesus stood and cried, saying, If any man thirst, let him come unto Me, and drink. He that believeth on Me...out of his belly shall flow rivers of living water. (But this spake He of the Spirit...)* (John 7:37-39).

His words pointed out how their water, or established practices of religion, was no longer adequate. Jesus gave living water, *chay mayim*. Just as He showed the Samaritan woman, His water doesn't need to be replenished, for Holy Spirit provides for that need.

FRESH WATER

John 4:14 says,

Whosoever drinketh of the water that I shall give him shall never thirst; but the water that I shall give him shall be in him a well of water springing up into everlasting life.

Even though this is Holy Spirit's function, most Christians are satisfied with not coming into the fullness of Holy Spirit. They don't understand how He works, so they choose not to go through this gate. Many even ridicule Holy Spirit manifestations or say those signs went out with the apostles in the Bible. Second Timothy 3:5 tells us some possess *"a form of godliness, but* [deny] *the power thereof"* instead of moving into all that's available to them. When we don't press into Holy Spirit, we settle for what's stale, rather than what's living.

When I was a child, our house had two different faucets for the cistern and the well. Though cistern water was clean enough to do dishes or bathe in, it wasn't fresh and drinkable like our well, which had clean, cool water like Aunt Cleo's. Biblical cisterns were also used for livestock and household chores; their water wasn't fresh or living.[13] Fountains are similar to springs and wells, for their water is fresh. Jeremiah 2:13 says,

For My people have committed two evils; they have forsaken Me the fountain of living waters, and hewed them out cisterns, broken cisterns, that can hold no water.

When we take natural sources of water from God's hand and try to do it ourselves, our efforts fall far short of what God wants for us. We've replaced true living water offered by Holy Spirit with man-made, broken systems of religion that Jeremiah calls "evil." Too many Christians are satisfied to drink from stagnant, nonproductive cisterns rather than from wells of living water. Cisterns are the old, stale covenant Jesus came to fulfill. Holy Spirit is the fountain of living water, the fresh well. Without Hezekiah's tunnel bringing forth *chay mayim*, Jerusalem would have died. We can never experience the fullness of what Christ ushered in with the New Covenant until we drink of the Spirit.

THE TOOLS

A few years ago, my daughter worked for a phone company and thought I needed to buy a Blackberry. It was a nice phone, but I'm not very technological, so it had more on it than I knew how to use. One day Jennifer said, "Mom, you're treating that Blackberry like it's a phone."

"Well, it is a phone," I quipped back.

"No, Mom, it's so much more than that. You can keep your calendar; you can text; you can use the alarm clock. You can access the internet; you can find directions; you can send emails. Mom, it's a Blackberry."

Unfortunately, most of us treat salvation like it is *just* salvation when it's so much more. Most churches we visit say, "Oh, yes, we believe in gifts of the Spirit," but they rarely use them. They don't seek the prophetic, which will allow them to see others' needs or know what the future holds for them so they can sidestep satan's snares. Paul admonishes the church at Corinth for having dissension among themselves and says they are *"behaving like mere men"* (1 Cor. 3:3 NKJV). When we engage in disputes about tools He's given us or refuse to press into what is available, we're acting like we're mere men and not those who have come into a deeper knowledge of God's plan. (We're acting like we're just phones and not Blackberries!)

Jesus said that when *"the Comforter, which is the Holy Ghost, whom the Father will send in My name* [comes], *He shall teach you all things..."* (John 14:26). We've been promised *"all things,"* but in reality most Christians have such mixed, negative feelings about Holy Spirit that they settle for a "few things," learning next to nothing about what's promised to them. They have the knowledge that God *can* do anything, but rarely do they experience the reality that He *will* do them. The understanding of His supreme power comes through intimately knowing Holy Spirit, the One for whom Jesus came to prepare the way. He said, *"I am the door: by Me if any man enter in, he shall be saved, and shall go in and out, and find pasture"* (John 10:9). Through Christ, we go into the wonderful door of salvation; like any door, it's just a passageway into a more fertile pasture. Things of the Holy Spirit that seem silly, scary, chaotic, or weird to so many, hold a limitless power to those who tap into His depths.

Activation of Holy Spirit and full surrender to Him bring growth, power, and essential tools for our progression into deeper spiritual things. God cares about all aspects of our lives—natural and spiritual, great and small. To make our experience richer, He's *"given unto us all things that pertain unto life and godliness"* (2 Pet. 1:3a). When Wade and I have ministered, many times we've seen God lengthen legs and do other dramatic miracles—but I remember one time when He revealed that someone had problems with his knuckles. A man came forward and was healed. He had gotten up that morning and couldn't clench his hand; his stiffened knuckles created an issue that affected his day at work. It seemed unimportant to some, but it was significant to him and God.

He cares about what we care about. Once He gave a word that He "cared even about someone's cat." As insignificant as that may seem, a woman was there whose cat had just died, and she was bottle feeding seven kittens. After the meeting she came to me and said she'd been overwhelmed, but God's individualized message to her had let her know she was important. God cares what happens to us, and often the small as well as big things say we live an overcoming lifestyle through Holy Spirit.

In the Fountain Gate, we begin to operate in gifts of the Spirit, which are alive and active today and given to *"profit withal"* (1 Cor. 12:7). God desires us to move in all nine gifts: words of wisdom, words of knowledge, faith, healing, miracles, prophecy, discerning of spirits, tongues, and interpretation of tongues (see 1 Cor. 12:4-10). Just as Jesus cared about meeting people's needs, we use the gifts to help others and show God's supremacy. We learned in the Fish Gate that we are to live to serve others, and here we often use our gifts to help others in dire circumstances. Those Holy Spirit gifts demonstrate power while making ours and others' Christian walks much richer. When people operate in those gifts, churches will see things occur they never thought possible.

POWER

One time when Wade and I were on a trip to Tennessee, the Lord gave me a dream about a lady named Sylvia. In it, she had on a pink sweater, and God told me to say, "Expect more!" This dream bothered me because I didn't know why I dreamt about a woman I barely knew or why I had such a specific message. The next day, we went to another Tennessee city where we would be ministering. In our hotel room that night, we had a powerful prayer session and could feel an anointing around the room. I was still bothered, though, about the dream from the night before and wondered if it had to do with our time here in this city. The next day, we went to a home to pray for a woman Wade knew who had incurable cancer. When she answered the door, she was being held up by her son and husband because the bottoms of her feet had been burned by strong cancer treatments.

She hugged Wade, chatted for a moment, and then turned to me. "It's so nice to meet you, Sylvia," she said. I was dumbfounded for a minute as Wade tried to smooth it over and tell her my name was Connie.

"I'm so sorry," she drawled with her thick Tennessee accent.

"I'm not," I whispered and smiled. There in her doorway, I told her about the dream and about the name of Sylvia. "I thought that dream may have been about today. I half expected you to show up wearing a pink sweater," I told her.

She just smiled at me. "It's in the wash!"

As we went inside and prayed for her, we realized what God was saying. Her chemo and radiation treatments had a lot of symptoms accompanying them. She had just accepted she had to live with them, but God had a message for her—"Expect more!" That day, as I sat on the floor in front of her couch and took hold of her ankles, she felt electricity go into them. By evening, she was well enough to go to church and walk on her own. After Wade preached, a great move of God came, and people were "slain in the Spirit." He asked me to pray with a lady who'd fallen onto the floor. As I grabbed her ankles, the woman on the floor jumped like she'd been touched by the paddles of life.

When that happened, the woman whom the Lord had touched that afternoon pointed and said to those around her, "See. See. What'd I tell you!" She turned to me and said enthusiastically, "Shock 'er again!"

I can't say enough about Holy Spirit and His work in Christians' lives because it's an innate part of my being. I was brought up in a Full Gospel church where Body ministry operated in nearly every service. For too long, we believers have relegated Holy Spirit to a corner and not allowed demonstrations of power through Him. Many things about Holy Spirit are controversial—for example, speaking in tongues. This feature of Holy Spirit is fought by most churches. I believe satan has convinced many Christians that speaking in tongues, praying in the Holy Spirit, and participating in Body ministry is wrong because he doesn't want them to find the accompanying power. Through praying in the Spirit, we not only can operate in a prophetic language, but we also can communicate exclusively with God. At times when we don't know how to pray, Holy Spirit can pray for us. Gifts are given to us to edify ourselves, the Church, and others, but if we don't use what's at our disposal, we're shortchanging everyone, and the enemy wins by default. Gifts are the ability of Jesus Christ (see 1 Cor. 12:4-10); the fruit of Holy Spirit is His character (see Gal. 5:22-23). That ability and character live within us in the Person of Holy Spirit. This alive Person, *chay mayim*, wants us to use what's rightfully ours to make our walk richer, more powerful, and more rewarding.

Through Holy Spirit, much untapped power remains at our disposal. That day in Tennessee, we had an experience with God's infusing might that created great consequence. It's like holding onto a hot electric source and aiming it at whatever you need. The first biblical reference to a fountain is found in Genesis 7:11 when the *"fountains of the great deep were broken up."* These were so intense they could be equated to earthquakes or tsunamis. The power of Holy Spirit is like this. It can create, fix, or reveal all manner of things if we allow it. Since Holy Spirit came to Earth, this power has raised the dead, healed the sick, and delivered the captive. It healed my sister of breast cancer, my daughter from chronic ear infections, and me from smallpox. But in our meetings, it also has healed knots on heads, toenails, and even belly buttons. Its great force creates power for all things, great and small.

EXOUSIA

The first type of power available is through Jesus' name. It brings authority to us just because we call on that name and believe. Before Holy Spirit came, disciples were healing and delivering in the powerful name of Jesus alone. *Strong's* calls this authority, "*exousia* – ability, privilege, force, capacity...authority...power."[14] Many examples show *exousia*.

- In Acts 5:4, Ananias and Sapphira had *exousia* to determine how much they gave.

- In Romans 9:21, the power the potter has to make the clay is *exousia*.

- In First Corinthians 9:4, we have *exousia* to eat and drink.

- In John 19:10, Pilate said he had *exousia* over Jesus.

- Jesus had *exousia* for choices He made while on Earth and said, *"No man taketh* [My life] *from Me, but I lay it down of Myself. I have power* [exousia] *to lay it down, and...to take it again..."* (John 10:18). Since He exercised *exousia* in making the choice to die and rise again for us, we can also exercise *exousia* in choosing Him, Holy Spirit, and all that comes with Them.

DUNAMIS

Just by His character, Holy Spirit has power, too. *Strong's Concordance* calls this power *dunamis*: "force, miraculous power, ability, abundance, ...might, miracle, power, strength, violence, mighty work."[15] There are also many powerful biblical examples of *dunamis*.

- Romans 15:13 says, *"Now the God of hope fill you with all joy and peace in believing, that ye may abound in hope, through the power* [dunamis] *of the Holy Ghost."*

- Jesus gave Holy Spirit and told His disciples they would *"receive power [dunamis], after that the Holy Ghost* [had] *come upon"* them (Acts 1:8).

- In Acts 6:8, Stephen did wonders and miracles with *dunamis.*

- In Acts 10:38, Jesus was anointed with *dunamis.*

- In Luke 22:69 God is described as having *dunamis,* and Romans 9:17 says His demonstration of power over Pharaoh was *dunamis.*

- In Romans 15:19, Paul preached from Jerusalem to Illyricum with *dunamis.*

- Luke 24:49 says, *"I send the promise of My Father upon you: but tarry ye in the city of Jerusalem, until ye be endued with power [dunamis] from on high."* Holy Spirit power has come now and has given us full access to *dunamis* and all that comes with it.

An amazing example of this *dunamis* power came one night when we were ministering. The Lord spoke a word of knowledge to a couple of ladies that someone was having problems with her heart. Another woman stood for prayer, and the ladies went to the back to minister to her. The Lord spoke to me to stretch out my hand from where I was sitting in the front and let electricity go from my fingers. I did that, and the ladies said they felt that tingling going through their bodies. What we found out a few days later was that another lady across the state had heart issues so severe she wore a monitor. At the same time we were praying for the lady in our meeting, the one across the state said she felt electricity go through her body. Twice, her heart monitor went crazy. She called the monitoring company who said her heart was fine and to take the monitor off. Both ladies were healed by power that came forth with the strength of earthquakes and tsunamis.

Jesus said, *"I give unto you power [exousia] to tread on serpents and scorpions, and over all the power [dunamis] of the enemy: and nothing shall by any means hurt you"* (Luke 10:19). This Scripture means satan also has *dunamis* power similar to Holy Spirit's. If all we had, however, were the *exousia* of Jesus' name, we could defeat satan in whatever he throws at us. Add to that the lightning-strength of *dunamis* we receive when we're baptized in Holy Spirit, and satan cannot prevail. We must assert it, and the Fountain Gate gives us that confidence. Satan is defeated by the unbeatable power and authority available to us.

CONCLUSION

I've heard people say that *exousia* and *dunamis* can be understood this way: *exousia* is the badge for the sheriff who has the authority to enforce the law, but *dunamis* is the gun he uses to back up his authority. Because of the *dunamis* Holy Spirit provides, we can expect many things to be added to our Christian walk: wisdom and knowledge (see Prov. 13:14); peace and comfort (see John 14:16); and fertile valleys through Him (see Isa. 41:18). We may cling to a promise for our children's salvation and prosperity; for He *"will pour* [His] *spirit upon* [our] *seed, and* [His] *blessing upon* [our] *offspring"* (Isa. 44:3b). Holy Spirit fills us at the Fountain Gate to take us into new levels in our Christian walk and give us long drinks to sustain us. The water is refreshing, comforting, fertile, and living. It's *chay mayim*. It has power to more than conquer whatever comes at us and bring light into dark times. We learn about this wondrous gift of Holy Spirit and all He has to give, here, in the Fountain Gate.

CHAPTER

7

THE WATER GATE: DEVOURING THE WORD

Moreover the Nethinims dwelt in Ophel, unto the place over against the water gate toward the east, and the tower that lieth out (Nehemiah 3:26).

Midwestern summers get really hot and humid. My childhood home didn't have air conditioning, but we had something even better to our minds—the creek. When the heat became unbearable, a trip down the hill to our refuge changed all our moods. Mossy rocks for sliding, gray clay squishing between our toes, and crawdads nipping at our feet made the experience more than refreshing. We splashed each other until we were exhausted but refreshed to endure whatever heat the day ahead would throw at us.

Water is crucial to our very essence. Earth is 70 percent water. The human body is 60 percent water in males, 55 percent water in females, and 70 percent in children.[1] Depending on conditions, one can last for more than a month without food but no more than a week without water.[2] Water not only invigorates us but also is important to our survival for drinking and bathing, so the next gate, the Water Gate, is also crucial. It represents one aspect of our walk that's more important than anything else—the Word. Christians need to be washed constantly with the water of the Word.

As we grow and experience more of the Lord, we can't neglect basic needs. Many of us go without God's Word all week until Sunday service; but when we do that we barely survive. Just as we need a constant supply of natural water, we need a perpetual dose of the Word to replenish what daily living depletes. A regular stream of spiritual water, His Word, allows us not just to survive but to thrive. The most growth we can experience in God is when we learn to dig into His Word. Not only does it refresh like a cool, country creek, but it also is meat that makes us grow.

As a child, I heard thousands of sermons, but all that preaching didn't give me as much nourishment as when I became an adult and had to prepare for a weekly teaching. Then, as I studied the Word, my hunger and thirst brought excitement and clarity. The Word gives sustenance for anything that comes along. Therefore, the Water Gate represents the Word of God, the main tool for strengthening and cleansing Christians.

THE WATER GATE

On our journey so far, we've learned varying degrees of the Word in each gate as we dug deeper in God. Now we get immersed in it. Some have thought, as I've taught this study, that the gates' placement seems reversed, but the Fountain Gate was put before the Water Gate on purpose. Since we went through the Fountain Gate, now we can better understand and appreciate the Water Gate. In this gate, the Word becomes alive because *chay mayim* of Holy Spirit has come fully into us and gives insight into God's Word to help us interpret it. As a matter of fact, the word for "water" in the featured scripture which describes this gate is *mayim*.[3] Remember *chay mayim*? This water of the Word is alive, too. In Hebrew, "*mayim* speaks of life, sustenance, fertility, blessing, and refreshing."[4] Don't all those describe the amazing Word of God? No one repaired this gate because the Word needs no fixing. This is the seventh gate; seven means perfection and completeness and is a consummate definition of the Word of God—perfect and complete.

The Water Gate was in the eastern wall by the Spring of Gihon. Remember, that's where living water was piped into Jerusalem. If extra water existed or if the Kidron Valley's water level was low, this gate resolved that need. Doesn't that also speak of the Word that helps in any situation—too much or too little? It gives balance, then stability. The *Nethinims,* which means "given or offered," were servants of the priests and Levites and dwelt beside the gate.[5] Likewise, the Word of God is our servant that goes forth from our mouths and *"prosper*[s] *in the thing whereto* [we] *sent it"* (Isa. 55:11c). When we repeat the Word, it acts as a servant to do whatever bidding we call it to do. *Ophel,* which means a "tower," was located on a high place in Jerusalem.[6] God's Word is above all else, a stronghold and fortress in our pursuit of Him.

Several passages make a connection between the Word and water. The definitive Scripture that connects those concepts is when we're told that we're sanctified when we are washed in water by His Word (see Eph. 5:26). The Isaiah 55:10-11 reference I just mentioned, says,

> *For as the rain cometh down, and the snow from heaven... [and] watereth the earth, and maketh it bring forth and bud, that it may give seed to the sower, and bread to the eater: so shall My word be that goeth forth out of My mouth: it shall not return unto Me void, but it shall accomplish that which I please, and it shall prosper in the thing whereto I sent it.*

Isaiah's simile of rain and word tells the results of falling rain—buds, seeds, bread. He compares that productivity to the results of the Word of God as it goes forth—it accomplishes and prospers. Just like the waters, the Word produces then brings about whatever it's been sent to do. Just like water maximizes the chance of seeds coming forth, so the Word waters the plantings of our faith and doesn't return void but produces what it's meant to.

Another interesting New Testament connection between water and the Word is in First John 5:6-8. Verse 7 lists three things that bear record in Heaven: *"the Father, the Word, and the Holy Ghost."* Verse 8 lists three parallel things that bear witness in earth: *"the Spirit, and the water, and the blood."* This passage is difficult to understand, and many have interpreted its meaning differently, so I'm not going to attempt what scholars disagree on. However, the interesting aspect of this passage for the Water Gate is the presentation in the New International Version. Where other translations list the three things separately, Father, Word, and Holy Ghost, then Spirit, water, and blood, the New International Version combines the information from verses 7 and 8. It says, *"There are three that testify: the Spirit, the water and the blood; and the three are in agreement"* (1 John 5:7-8 NIV). This merging of these verses carries the implication that the water and the Word are the same.

THE GODHEAD

As I've contemplated the placement of these gates, I realized that separating Holy Spirit from the Word was impossible. The Godhead is all one: *"the Father, the Word, and the Holy Ghost: and these three are one"* (1 John 5:7b). The Word doesn't operate as an island but rather as a partnership to bring divine revelation to us. Jesus said, *"I will pray the Father, and He will give you another Helper, that He may abide with you forever"* (John 14:16 NKJV). Jesus didn't leave so we could be alone with Holy Spirit. The plan for Holy Spirit to come and be our "Helper" was a joint effort among the Father, Son, and Holy Spirit. In this verse the word *another* is *allos,* "one besides, another of the same kind."[7] So, the Helper we got wasn't another *in place of,* but rather another *in addition to* Jesus. They're all one, and when *"our gospel came* [it wasn't] *in word only, but also in power, and in the Holy Ghost"* (1 Thess. 1:5a). So, the power of Holy Spirit and the Word work together, inextricably bound, to do a work in us.

The Bible, God's very words, is the consummate authority to base our lives upon. Second Timothy 3:16-17 says,

> *"All scripture is given by inspiration of God, and is profitable for doctrine, for reproof, for correction, for instruction in righteousness: That the man of God may be perfect, thoroughly furnished unto all good works"* as he grows toward his destiny.

The word *inspiration* is the Greek word *theopneustos*, "divinely breathed in—given by inspiration of God."[8] Just as He created the heavens *"by the breath of his mouth"* (Ps. 33:6), so did He create Scriptures. *"For the prophecy came not in old time by the will of man: but holy men of God spake as they were moved by the Holy Ghost"* (2 Pet. 1:21). As a matter of fact, though the Bible was penned by humans, "even the words used in the giving of the Bible...were planned by the Holy Spirit."[9] That's why a study of the original words used in a Scripture is so important. So the Water Gate is a continuation of the Fountain Gate because Holy Spirit authored the Word of God.

Part of the Godhead is Jesus, who *is* the Word. John tells us that in multiple places: *"In the beginning was the Word, and the Word was with God, and the Word was God"* (John 1:1), that *"the Word was made flesh, and dwelt among us"* (John 1:14a), and that *"His name is called The Word of God"* (Rev. 19:13b). That Word came to bring light into this dark world (see John 8:12) so those living in that darkness didn't have to anymore (see John 12:46). By His character, He defines the Word— *"the way, the truth, and the life"* (John 14:6). He was the sacrifice that cleansed, but not like in the Old Testament where the washing happened each year. He was the ultimate sacrifice that cleansed *"once* [and] *for all"* (Heb. 10:10). As He works through His Word, He brings sanctification into us.

LIVING WATER

Six hundred references to water occur in the Bible.[10] Genesis 1:2 first mentions water when God's spoken word moved on the face of the waters to create light. The water of the Word also brings light to us. Water is valuable in this culture since rain is scarce and droughts are common. Because of erratic rains, Middle Easterners rely on wells, cisterns, and especially springs since they're living water (*chay mayim*).[11] Those waters are life-sustaining, and we, too, must dig in where we can imbibe the clear Word of God. Living water from the Spring of Gihon in Jerusalem's natural spring gushes forth extra water each day.[12] Have you ever been in a time when you were going through a dry spell and needed God to give extra direction just as Jerusalem needed extra water from the Spring of Gihon? Often that additional amount comes by seeking Him through His Word. Both Holy Spirit and the Word burst forth in our lives, too; we need to cherish both like a spring in the desert.

Living water rushed out in Kadesh when Moses struck the rock (see Num. 20:2-13). In Exodus 15:25 bitter *"waters were made sweet."* This became living water. That living water we discovered at the Fountain Gate is part of the living Word at this gate. Because we experienced Holy Spirit there, we're able to read the Word with His insight, and He gives direction for whatever quandary we encounter. Because this Word is living, it can be our tool for whatever we must accomplish.

That living Word creates excitement. On the road to Emmaus, Jesus, after He was resurrected, quoted the Word to Cleopas and another person. Later they said, *"Did not our heart burn within us, while He talked with us by the way, and while He opened to us the Scriptures?"* (Luke 24:32). Have you ever felt or seen that burning occur in a church service when someone was preaching or teaching the Word of God that had come alive? Listeners sit spellbound because hearts do *"burn within"* as Scripture becomes more than just black or red words on a page. One night during Bible Study as Wade taught about ministering and praying from the mercy seat, Sheri, a lady who regularly attends our meetings and workshops, jumped up and excitedly clapped. Everyone looked at her.

"I get it," she said. "I understand why my prayers aren't always answered." She sat and beamed the rest of the evening because of the Word that had come alive to her.

The unsaved often argue that Christians are basing their lives on precepts in God's Word, a book that's thousands of years old. They say it's out of step with the world today. I beg to differ! Hebrews 4:12 says,

> *The word* [logos] *of God is quick, and powerful, and sharper than any two-edged sword, piercing even to the dividing asunder of soul and spirit, and of the joints and marrow, and is a discerner of the thoughts and intents of the heart.*

This Scripture tells us we aren't allowing a dead book to guide us. How often have you read a Scripture that suddenly comes alive so you see it differently from every other time you've studied it? Like Holy Spirit, the Word is *chay mayim* that can live in, guide, and work for us. God's Word is so powerful and essential, David said, *"I will...praise Thy name for Thy loving-kindness and for Thy truth: for Thou hast magnified Thy word above all Thy name"* (Ps. 138:2). As important as the Lord's redemptive names listed in Chapter 3 are, His Word is even more precious.

David declares that the Word of God is a delight for us. He says God's Word is *"sweeter also than honey and the honeycomb"* (Ps. 19:10b). If we think of the sweetest treat we can, God's Word far surpasses that indulgence, for it's not only rich, but also filling. David later repeats, *"How sweet are Thy words unto my taste! yea, sweeter than honey to my mouth!"* (Ps. 119:103). Hebrew tradition says as a Jewish child learned Scriptures, his parents would give him honey as a reward. This created an association of sweetness to the Word of God.[13] The Word can be sweet to us, too, if we chew, linger, and savor its richness.

CLEANSING

Many important reasons exist for us to eat, drink, sleep, and breathe His Word. As I said before, a connection between water and cleansing is stated in Ephesians: *"He might sanctify and cleanse* [us] *with the washing of water by the word"* (Eph. 5:26). Because we're in this living water, that word is now a *rhema*, a word that gives us a timely direction for something we need to know in our lives now. Since we've gone through the Fountain Gate, Holy Spirit now helps us get *rhemas* by hearing His voice, getting a "now" word, and knowing His secrets. He renews or cleanses us *and "saved us by the washing of regeneration, and renewing of the Holy Ghost"* (Titus 3:5). Again, it's a joint effort—Holy Spirit renews through Jesus. We became separated from the world at the beginning of our journey, so He still wants us not to be *"conformed to this world: but...transformed by the renewing of your mind, that ye may prove what is that good, and acceptable, and perfect, will of God"* (Rom. 12:2). Here in this gate we can find what His will is through the Word and thus renew our minds.

In biblical times, Hebrews cleansed themselves from things that could pollute them: touching the dead, childbirth, menstruation, body fluids, sexual activity, animal sacrifices, forbidden foods, skin diseases, or contact with lepers.[14] Cleansing was so important that specific rituals were performed for bathing and washing food, utensils, and clothing.[15] Jesus' baptism by John represented cleansing, as did Pilate's washing of his hands (see Matt. 3:13-15; 27:24). Jesus, however, challenged the idea of cleansing when He showed that religion stressed outward cleansing while the inside of a person remained unchanged. He told Nicodemus he must be born again with water baptism and Holy Spirit to clean both body and spirit (see John 3:1-21). He rebuked those who cleaned *"the outside of the cup and the platter;* [while the] *inward part is full of...wickedness"* (Luke 11:39). We live in a culture that elevates outward beauty; that attitude even permeates the Church. Jesus said it's what's inside a person that really matters, and we must be cleansed from what pollutes us, too. As we renew our minds, we conform to how Jesus wants us to be, both inside and out.

Today, He's still more interested in what we are inside than outside. Paul reminds us that we should *"look not at the things which are seen, but at the things which are not seen"* (2 Cor. 4:18a), for those are eternal. He says that this cleansing, or renewing, happens constantly to *"the inward man* [who] *is being renewed day by day"* (2 Cor. 4:16) while the outer man just grows a little older each day. The proof of that is in my mirror each morning!

In our journey through the gates so far, a lot of our Christian walk has been spent on ridding ourselves of things that are displeasing to God and could hold us back from going into His fullness. At this gate, as we spend more and more time in His Word, the process becomes more refined and we're *"clean through the word which* [He has] *spoken"* to us (John 15:3). We delve into those words and find the best way to be cleansed is to be "sanctif[ied] ...*through* [God's] *truth:* [His] *word is truth"* (John 17:17). That's the type of truth not driven by doctrines or others' feelings about what God wants us to strive for. David asks and then answers this question: How shall a *"young man cleanse his way? by taking heed thereto according* to *Thy word"* (Ps. 119:9). This gate is another piece of the sanctification process that other gates began in us. As we dig into Scripture, we become more familiar with God's Word and are *"sanctified by the word of God and prayer"* (1 Tim. 4:5). Cleansing uses the yardstick of the Word to measure right and wrong for our walk. It lets us hear what God is saying in His Word while Holy Spirit helps us apply it to our lives.

FERTILITY

Remember how Isaiah said the Word would produce results just like the rain? This Word brings satisfaction when *"every one that thirsteth, come[s]...to the waters"* (Isa. 55:1a). It brings fertility when we take up residence in it. Joel 3:18 says fertile mountains, hills, and rivers will be in Judah and a fountain will flow from God's house. We walked in fertility in the first six gates, but now we find richness that comes only through knowing Scripture. Isaiah 58:11 says,

> *The Lord shall guide thee continually, and satisfy thy soul in drought, and make fat thy bones: and thou shalt be like a watered garden, and like a spring of water, whose waters fail not.*

Sometimes we're caught up in the leanness of our lives and need something to bring us fertility. When we need direction and fat bones, for a change, Scripture can give it. I know people who go to the Word in their own time of drought, and the Lord gives them promises to hold onto. Some just open their Bibles, and God speaks to them. Then they find their deserts transformed into a well-watered place. He gives us fertility to rest and peace in our storm when *"He leadeth* [us] *beside the still waters"* (Ps. 23:2b).

Often when my life has been in a dry place, delving into the Word has opened up springs of water to create fertility for me again. Once, bombarded by marital, financial, work, church, and children problems, I couldn't see any way for things to work out. As I did my devotions, I found Scriptures that spoke promises to me about my desperate situations. Those nuggets that fed my parched soul became so massive, I wanted to hold onto them to chew on whenever I needed encouragement. I made a journal of those Scriptures and read them repeatedly until God brought me through my time of despair.

In the years since, I still look at the Scripture journal to find direction or promises. Isaiah 43:19b says, *"I will even make a way in the wilderness, and rivers in the desert."* I was truly in a wilderness from which (at times) it looked like I couldn't escape, yet His Word became the water that nurtured me and made a way for me to get my bearings again. It gave me hope for desperation and rivers for dried gullies to sustain me. I have since shared my Scripture journal with many who were going through similar adversities, and they, too, found comfort in those Scriptures that fed my parched soul. There is a place of fertility when we *"attend to* [His] *words...* [and] *keep them in the midst of* [our] *heart. For they are life unto those that find them, and health to all their flesh"* (Prov. 4:20-22). It brought life back into me and a situation that satan wanted dead for me.

MATURITY

This Word also brings maturity into the lives of Christians. Paul said, *"We henceforth* [should] *be no more children, tossed to and fro, and carried about with every wind of doctrine...* [but should] *grow up into Him in all things..."* (Eph. 4:14-15). Many aren't strong enough to withstand various winds that come along because they're planted in unstable places and haven't taken up abode in His Word. Even in a Christian setting, some lead sheep astray because weaker ones don't possess the solidity needed to stand. David concurred with those sentiments and spoke in terms of water. Psalm 1:2-3 says,

> *His delight is in the law of the Lord; and in His law doth he meditate day and night. And he shall be like a tree planted by the rivers of water, that bringeth forth his fruit in his season; his leaf also shall not wither; and whatsoever he doeth shall prosper.*

So, the result of meditating on the Word constantly is stability, fruit, life, and prosperity. The Hebrew use of "meditate" is different from ours. As they mediated, they softly hummed to keep from being distracted away from the Word. As they hummed, they got "lost in communion with God."[16] When we dip our roots into the river of the Word with single-mindedness, we have to become more stable and prosperous. Joshua confirms the necessity of *"meditat*[ing]...*day and night"* on the Word (Josh. 1:8). This *meditate* means that you shall "be constantly in."[17] I can always tell those who have put their roots into the water constantly because they have more depth and scriptural understanding than others. When we plant ourselves by the water and put our roots down deep into the Word, we won't droop but will grow as we're nurtured by the Truth. With our roots in His Word, God can feed and lead us.

Moses said a man should study God's Word *"all the days of his life: that he may learn to fear the Lord...* [and] *to keep all the words of this law..."* (Deut. 17:19). True wisdom and growth come as we learn more about the Lord and His expectations through the Word. God doesn't want us to stay babies. If our own children remained infants forever, something would be wrong with their development. Christian children also need to become adults sometime. When we were in the Sheep Gate, we were children. Every gate since then, however, should have been a maturing process. Unfortunately, some Christians came to the Sheep Gate many years ago but never grew any deeper in the Lord. Usually, those are the ones who haven't spent time with the Lord or in His Word. God gives His Word so *"the man of God may be perfect, thoroughly furnished unto all good works"* (2 Tim. 3:17). *Strong's* defines the word *perfect* as *artios,* "complete."[18] God wants us "completely ready to meet the demands of discipleship."[19] Something's missing when we don't get into the Word.

LOGOS

Our maturing comes when we understand various levels of His Word. First is the *logos,* the written Word of God, which is always and forever. We began to get into the Word at the Old Gate, but now we understand our need not just to read but to devour it. Reading the *logos* is crucial because Scripture is what we measure everything by in our Christian walk. *Logos* is solid if we read it and then do what it says. Jesus said, *"Heaven and earth shall pass away, but My words* [logos] *shall not pass away"* (Matt. 24:35). Nothing that happens in the Earth—from the economy to natural disasters—can change what the Bible says; therefore, we can trust it all will work into God's plan. Second Peter 3:5-7 says this Word was part of the creative process, has been vital since before the Earth was formed, and is still crucial today. It's the stability needed to make us grow stronger in Him.

As I said earlier, this *logos* was given to us in the form of His Son, Jesus; for *"in the beginning was the Word [logos]"* (John 1:1a). This Word was at one with water when He calmed the storm and walked across the sea. He showed its prosperity when He provided coins from a fish's mouth and twice helped disciples with their catch of fish. He taught about its cleansing power as He was baptized and washed the disciples' feet. Water was where and how this *logos* operated. At the Water Gate, the *logos* is crucial because it's our foundation. It's Jesus. The *logos* brings many things into our lives. In Acts 10:44, we read that *"while Peter yet spake these words, the Holy Ghost fell on all them which heard the word [logos]."* Just listening to the Word activated Holy Spirit in them. Peter saw how important *logos* was to growth and said that *"as newborn babes, [we should] desire the sincere milk of the word [logos], that [we] may grow thereby"* (1 Pet. 2:2). Then as we mature from a newborn babe to other levels of development, the constant wisdom of the Word gives spiritual direction (see Col. 3:16) and power (see 1 Cor. 4:20). It's the tool by which God *drew us* and thus will shape us by guidelines He's set forth in His Word (James 1:18a).

RHEMA

The other level of the Word of God we need to rely on is the *rhema,* a word from the Word. Though we already have some *logos* in us from the other gates, since we've now come through the Fountain Gate and been filled with the Spirit, we can better comprehend the *rhema,* the proceeding Word of God. In other words, it's a timely word for now. Again, that doesn't mean we haven't received timely words at other places along the journey, but now Holy Spirit is leading us into all truths; we can receive more direction to let us lead an overcoming lifestyle. Until Holy Spirit gives His guidance, *rhemas* aren't as alive for us. Coupling that *logos* with Holy Spirit makes that now word come alive in our personal lives.

When John 1:1 speaks of Jesus, all of these uses of "Word" translate to *logos*; therefore, Jesus is the *logos*. Holy Spirit is referred to as a "Comforter," *parakletos*—"intercessor, consoler, advocate."[20] In John 14:26b (NKJV) Jesus says Holy Spirit *"will teach you all things, and bring to your remembrance all things that* [Jesus] *said to you."* That means that Jesus, the *logos,* coupled with Holy Spirit, the *rhema,* brings recall, revelation, and understanding of the Word while producing truth and direction. That word, then, is spoken for our circumstances today, not just 3,000 years ago. We gain understanding and applicability to our lives because this is a Now God, who, though He always was and always will be, is *I Am,* not *I Was. Rhemas* are a perfect example of living water with freshness and revelation flowing into us. Romans 10:17 says faith grows because it *"cometh by hearing...the* [rhema] *of God."* Our faith grows because of what a *rhema produces.*

I understand how a *rhema* works because my mother operated so fluently in them when God gave her a prophetic action, which she called God's M.O., His method of operation. Once I was visiting her and my dad in Arizona during the holidays when we received news that a friend of hers was going from Phoenix to a hospital in Texas. She had cancer that had progressed so far she was being sent to the Texas facility and was never expected to return from there. My mother got one of her "M.O." expressions.

"I know if I can just put my hands on her, she'll be OK."

"That can't happen," my dad told her. "She's going straight from Phoenix to Texas."

"If I can put my hands on her, she'll be OK." I knew better than to argue with Mom when she had a *rhema.* I didn't think much else about it until later in the afternoon when the phone rang. The lady's doctor had allowed her to come home for the weekend to spend her last Christmas with her family. Mom would be able to lay her hands on her.

We drove the 25 miles to her house, and Mom, Dad, Grandpa, and I went in to pray. Emaciated, weak, and pale, she was lying on a bed in the corner of the room. As soon as I saw her condition, I realized it wouldn't be my faith that brought healing into her body. Mom, however, knew what she knew because she had memorial pillars from what God had done in the past when she responded to her *rhemas*. We all prayed and left. After the weekend, the lady went on to Texas. News came quickly. Not only was she not dying; she was cancer-free. She came back home soon, got stronger, and finally was back to normal. Mom knew that promises for healing come through the *logos,* but once she'd gotten a *rhema* to hold onto, she just had to believe and act on the revelation. Then God brought about results. Healing came because of that *rhema* and her obedience.

Those words, part of your Holy Spirit infilling, are timely and appropriate for your "now" situation. Since Holy Spirit and His gifts dwell in us, we can get a *rhema* by reading the Bible, hearing prophetic words, or having personal revelations. Once we were filled with Holy Spirit in the Fountain Gate, we became in tune with His *rhema*. As when God spoke the Earth into existence, a *rhema* is God speaking something into existence in our lives, for *"through faith we understand that the worlds were framed by the word* [rhema] *of God"* (Heb. 11:3a). God used a *rhema* to bring His Son to earth, for *"Mary said, Behold the handmaid of the Lord; be it unto me according to thy word* [rhema]..." (Luke 1:38). Hebrews 1:3 says Jesus came through a *"word* [rhema] *of His power, when He had by Himself purged our sins, sat down on the right hand of the Majesty on high."* A *rhema* can set into motion phenomenal things.

Remember when Jesus told the disciples to let down their nets again after they had fished all night without catching anything? Simon told the Lord that though they had caught nothing, *"at* [Jesus'] *word* [rhema] *I will let down the net"* (Luke 5:5). That *rhema* from the Lord plus the disciples' obedience brought about results. When we're unsure about how to proceed, a *rhema* can give direction, and we, like Simon, can fill our boats with fish instead of coming away empty. *Rhemas* free us to bring His will into manifestation through our own obedience. With the words we give others or receive ourselves, we often must wait upon the Lord for confirmation and His timing. But if we seek Him and then stand, He'll be faithful.

Paul says, *"Let him that is taught in the word [rhema] communicate unto him that teacheth in all good things"* (Gal. 6:6). When we receive a *rhema* as a word of knowledge or wisdom, it's incumbent upon us not only to hold it as our personal promise, but also to share what God has given to direct others. Often, our willingness to follow through with His revelation determines how much God can trust us with His treasures and how often He'll give them to us in the future. A *rhema* brings life, for *"man shall not live by bread alone, but by every word [rhema] that proceedeth out of the mouth of God"* (Matt. 4:4). As important as daily food is to our body, this word is just as crucial to sustaining us and others because when God gives us that *rhema*, it's a done deal. Therefore, when things happen that bring pain and problems into our lives or when we just need direction, holding on to the *rhema*, our promise from God, can bring peace and victory. So, just as the *logos* is essential to our Christian walk, so is the *rhema*—and both sustain us.

Rhemas don't diminish *logos*, for the written Word is what we judge everything else by. Often we may receive a word from another person whom we trust and know can hear from God. However, all people who operate in Holy Spirit are human beings, imperfect and still learning about their giftings. Therefore, Scripture says we need to judge those words, and the best way to judge the *rhema* is by its alignment with the *logos*. If it violates the inviolable Word, it's wrong, plain and simple. A *rhema*, however, based on *logos* given to us through Holy Spirit is truly God speaking into a current situation. It's the Ephesians 6:17 sword of the Spirit with which we battle and pray in Holy Spirit. Then we stand on that M.O.

Wade's and my ministry deals with *rhemas* frequently because God reveals His will to us so often in words of wisdom and knowledge. Once I was praying, and God brought to my mind Wade's daughters, both of whom were having problems conceiving. Suddenly, the Lord put into my spirit that we needed to start praying daily and claiming that life would be brought forth. We did that faithfully for several weeks until we received word both of them had become pregnant within two weeks after our God-directed prayers began. About eight months later, Wade became a grandpa three times in the same night after both daughters gave birth and one of the girls had twins! *Rhemas* that we speak and act upon call into existence God's will with His *now* words.

CONCLUSION

My mother was a strong woman who understood both the *logos* and *rhema*. As she read the Word, God brought intense revelations to her. The *now* word, though, operated just as fluently in her many other times in our lives. One day when an icy snowstorm canceled our Oxford, Ohio, school, my siblings and I were sledding on the hill by our house. Mom was home praying when suddenly she was pierced by a knowing she had to get us away from that hill. She called for us in a tone that let us know we were to come home right away without any "back talking" or "lollygagging." As we got to the kitchen door and were shaking off the snow from our boots, behind us, we heard a bang like a dissonant drum. The electric line had broken beneath the weight of the ice and fallen—right onto the place where we'd been. It burned so long that forever while we lived there, a ridge was indented into the top of that hill. Her obedience to God's voice saved all our lives that day—and many other times when He came to her or Dad with a word. They both learned early in their Christian journey with God that eating the Word and listening to that *rhema* gave them an overcoming lifestyle.

Romans 1:16 says, *"I am not ashamed of the gospel of Christ: for it is the power [dunamis] of God unto salvation to every one that believeth...."* The Water Gate is symbolic of the Word of God, washing our lives and sanctifying us. Holy Spirit makes God's *logos* alive to us, bringing growth, cleansing, refreshing, direction, empowerment, fertility, and sustenance. His *rhema* takes that Word and applies it to our lives right now. Joshua 1:8 says, as we meditate on the word constantly, it will make our *"way prosperous, and then* [we] *shalt have good success.*

His Word is total, perfect, and complete. Just like Jesus.

CHAPTER

8

The Horse Gate:
Doing Warfare

From above the horse gate repaired the priests, every one over against his house (Nehemiah 3:28).

Do you remember the old schoolyard bully? He's the one who made your life miserable every time you showed up. He'd ridicule you, challenge you, fight you, or even steal your lunch money, but if you ever took action against him, he'd "whup you good." You dreaded recess or walking to school because you knew it would be the same thing every day. However, then hope arrived in the form of an older brother, neighbor, cousin, or friend. That changed the dynamics of your problem because the bully knew he could no longer push you around: now you had someone who would fight those battles for you. You had someone who would always win, and even when he wasn't there, just mentioning his name would send the bully running.

That's what happens at this point in our Christian experience. We've gained strength in the Lord, so now there comes an inevitable time when we must do battle. Satan is an unworthy adversary who taunts, steals, and throws everything he can at us. Then he tells us we have no hope or makes us feel guilty because we fell for his tricks. However, our friend *"that sticketh closer than a brother"* fights battles we simply can't win on our own (Prov. 18:24). We'll always be the victor as long as we realize that when we do battle with satan, God is the predetermined winner. By ourselves, we can't fight the bully who fights us. Therefore, the best thing we can do is to let our loving Father take care of the battle. Our part in the process is simply to believe and obey. Then, we don't just eke out a victory, but *"we are more than conquerors through Him that loved us"* (Rom. 8:37). The key phrase in that passage is *"through Him."*

THE HORSE GATE

We learned dependence on the Shepherd back at the Sheep Gate, and we must rely on Him still though our battles are harder now. We gained maturity at other gates that allowed us to grow stronger so now we can win skirmishes. The Old Gate gave knowledge of God and His Word and erected memorial pillars that gave us confidence He'll come through for us now just as He did then. Our time in the Valley and Dung Gates let us battle through hardships and work on our character, and strength grew each time we overcame another stronghold. In the Fountain Gate, we took on the ally of Holy Spirit and received tools that can give us a heads-up about satan's plans. Now, because we learned the Word in the Water Gate, we *"know the truth, and the truth shall make* [us] *free"* from the tormentor (John 8:32). It's fitting we should come to the Horse Gate immediately after the Fountain and Water Gates. We're armed now with everything an overcomer needs—Holy Spirit and God's Word as tools of warfare. We're destined to succeed through Him.

The first reference to horses occurs in Genesis 49:17 when we read that the tribe of *"Dan* [which means judgment or he that judgeth] *shall be a serpent by the way, an adder in the path, that biteth the horse heels, so that his rider shall fall backward."* Whenever a serpent is mentioned in the Bible, it usually describes satan, who judges our weaknesses and nips at us to get us to fall back into our old ways. This is a constant battle for many—he appraises where he can get a foothold then slips in through the crack. As you know, battles we fight are often for ourselves or our families, so we need to be ever vigilant to guard our homes. At this gate, even priests made repairs beyond the Horse Gate in front of their own houses. Each of us as kings and priests is responsible for warfare for our own houses. Sometimes that's our most important God-given responsibility—to repair or keep our families. If going to battle on behalf of ourselves and family members were the only warfare we did, it would be worth it; however, a Christian is called to much more.

The Horse Gate was on the east side of the wall and overlooked the Kidron Valley. The gate probably got its name either because it was beside the stables or because it was near the palace. It was alluded to in Second Kings when evil was destroyed there as Queen Athaliah (daughter of Ahab and Jezebel) was killed. She and her husband Jehoram had murdered his six brothers and reinstated Baal worship, a religion more heinous than others because of its sexual promiscuity and sacrifice of children by fire. When Jehoram died, Ahaziah (their son) reigned with his mother and made Baal worship the accepted religion. When he died, she ruled alone and killed all heirs except Joash, a baby whom her sister hid. When he was six, Joash's followers overthrew Athaliah and *"she went by the way by the which the horses came into the king's house: and there was she slain"* (2 Kings 11:16). Slaying evil is part of our Christian experience. Here at the Horse Gate, just like with Athaliah, we actively engage in warfare to eject satan from areas where he's buffeted us.

Battles are such an important part of a Christian's life; the Bible mentions warfare or battle nearly 400 times. My husband often says that usually we're in one of three places: in a battle, just finishing one, or going into one. Though some battles seem devastating, they're preparing us for harder ones that are coming, for *"if thou hast run with the footmen, and they have wearied thee, then how canst thou contend with horses?"* (Jer. 12:5a). That doesn't make us feel better when we know God is saying, "Relax. Things are going to get worse," but this is all part of the refining process as we move toward our Assignment Gate. How can God entrust us with the deeper things we'll do for His Kingdom if we can't succeed in minor skirmishes along the way?

HORSES AS SYMBOLS OF WARFARE

On Saturdays Wade and I like to get jobs done around the house. Many of those require our being in the kitchen and dining room, so we turn on the TV to pass the time while we work. Saturdays, it seems, are when our favorite channels broadcast two types of *his* preferred movies—cowboys and war. In both genres, one staple prop emerges: horses. Whether John Wayne is forging his way across the plains fighting the Indians or ancient Egyptians are speeding in their fancy chariots into battle, horses are an icon we equate with warring. Biblically, they're an important symbol, too; they are mentioned more than 200 times in the Bible. Many Scriptures refer to them as objects of war, so it's fitting this gate uses that analogy.

Horses have a few traits that parallel us and our spiritual warfare.[2] They possess swiftness and endurance like that which God develops in each of us. Like a sheep, a horse knows its Master's voice and is ready, just as we are, to do His bidding when He calls. However, horses can be stubborn and require being broken. "Hammerheads" like me are not to be *"as the horse, or as the mule, which have no understanding: whose mouth must be held in with bit and bridle..."* for discipline (Ps. 32:9). The Master's chastisement—*"a whip for the horse, a bridle for the ass, and a rod for the fool's back"*—makes the horse ready to be useful in war (Prov. 26:3). They usually pulled chariots or bore warriors into battle and thus symbolized military strength.[3] As horses represent victory in battle, they also represent spiritual power.

The might of Elisha's ministry is demonstrated by horses. When he and Elijah were traveling together, *"there appeared a chariot of fire, and horses of fire...and Elijah went up by a whirlwind into heaven"* (2 Kings 2:11b). Then, when Elisha's servant was afraid of the Syrians, Elisha said,

> *Fear not: for they that be with us are more than they that be with them.... And the Lord opened the eyes of the young man; and he saw: and, behold, the mountain was full of horses and chariots of fire round about Elisha* (2 Kings 6:16-17).

Another time, when Syria had surrounded Samaria and cut them off from their source of supply, people became so hungry that mothers boiled and ate their own children. After Elisha's prophecy, God made Syrians *"to hear a noise of chariots, and a noise of horses, even the noise of a great host"* (2 Kings 7:6a). They fled, and God's people were able to eat the spoils. For Elisha, horses represented God's supernatural intercession, provision, might, and deliverance as he went to battle with God's leading. The same is true when we go forth with God's direction and might.

BIBLICAL PROMISES

Since we have travelled through other gates before this one, we should understand our rights in Christ before we enter the battlefield. That knowledge of sure victory in Him comes as we learn His promises in the *logos*, make them our *rhema*, and then cling to them.

- *"No weapon that is formed against thee shall prosper; and every tongue that shall rise against thee in judgment thou shalt condemn"* (Isa. 54:17a).

- He desires that we *"mayest prosper and be in health, even as* [our] *soul prospereth"* (3 John 2).

- We *"shall not die, but live, and declare the works of the Lord"* (Ps. 118:17).

- We are the *"head, and not the tail"* (Deut. 28:13).

- *"All* [our] *children shall be taught of the Lord; and great shall be the peace of* [our] *children"* (Isa. 54:13).

- *"I have been young, and now am old; yet have I not seen the righteous forsaken, nor his seed begging bread"* (Ps. 37:25).

As we learn promises such as these and grow confident in God's ability, each gate expands our trust in Him. We can do warfare by the Word and know the outcome in advance. As those promises become personal to us as a *rhema*, God's responsible for the results He's assured us of. They're powerful weapons in our war arsenal.

When Wade and I pastored, a young couple with a little boy came to our church from several miles away. Some years before, the mother had been unable to bear children, so she joined a Christian support group that helped pray one another to pregnancies. As each woman conceived by God's miraculous hand, this woman rejoiced for others. Then she became pregnant herself and delivered a little boy. For an added blessing, God gave them another baby—a little girl who was now a toddler.

We had never seen that baby because they had lost custody of her. When she was born, she stayed in the hospital for quite some time because of a physical issue. When her parents were finally allowed to take her home, they noticed she cried out whenever they handled her. When they took her back to the hospital the next day, the doctors discovered she had a broken rib. Because of the injury, child services took the baby away despite the fact that the rib was already healing so it had to have been done while she was in the hospital. Many prayers went up, but ongoing court battles denied the parents' guardianship. The little girl was nearly two years old and had been in her parents' custody only one night.

One evening, after they'd been going to our church for a while, the mother frantically called. Through devastated tears, she managed to say that during their visit that day to court, the judge had decided to put the baby up for adoption. As I listened, suddenly the Lord put into my spirit a *rhema* about the barren Shunammite woman (see 2 Kings 4:8-37). The man of God had promised her a baby, and God had been true to His Word. Therefore, when her child died a few years later, she refused to give him up and sought the prophet's help, for she knew God wouldn't take her child of promise. That night, as this devastated woman was sobbing into the phone, it came into my spirit He wouldn't take this barren mother's child of promise either. Because I knew His *logos*, I could apply it as a *rhema*. As I did, I felt Holy Spirit's power come into that room. We prayed with confidence that the Lord would accomplish what this godly woman had believed for these many months. Shortly afterward, the parents had one more court appearance to determine the baby's fate. When they arrived, the judge had changed; the new one gave them full custody. God has promises for us to lean on, but if we don't know His Word, how can we do warfare that will produce Kingdom results?

WARFARE

The only way anyone can learn warfare is to go to battle. David was a mighty man of God who fought many successful battles both before and during his time as king. However, he allowed himself to become weary of the battle. Once, *"at the time when kings go forth to battle"* (2 Sam. 11:1),

David stayed home instead of going to war with his men. He went onto his roof and saw Bathsheba bathing on the roof across the way. Because he'd neglected his battle time, he was in a position to lust after and begin an affair with her. After she was pregnant, he orchestrated her husband's death, which impacted his family's lives forever. David opened himself to temptation because he wasn't at the place of battle. We can't gain our victory if we don't go to war, and then we're susceptible to satan.

Most warfare is inside our minds where we struggle with finding God's will and standing in faith. Victory comes through knowing God will prevail if we seek Him and find the *rhema* for the battle as we push past our own minds to get the mind of Christ. In Second Chronicles 20, Jehoshaphat, king of Judah went against Ammon, Moab, and the Horites of Mount Seir. Those armies surrounded Jerusalem and left no hope of victory. Jehoshaphat put his trust in the Lord and prayed, *"In Thine hand is there not power and might, so that none is able to withstand Thee?"* (2 Chron. 20:6b). God answered Jehoshaphat through a Levite upon whom the Spirit of the Lord came, and said, *"The battle is not yours, but God's"* (2 Chron. 20:15). Instead of fretting and fighting to gain victory by his own military prowess, Jehoshaphat sent worshipers ahead to proclaim God's goodness and victory. This strategy so confused Judah's enemies they killed each other. The spoil was enormous; it took three days for God's people to pick it up. Three is the number of completeness, and a complete victory is the only kind God gives. This is a template for battles we fight. When we know the battle belongs to God, we can worship for our victory in advance. Then we can rest and see it unfold in His way and time.

As I said, my mom called this revelation of the Lord's battle plan His M.O. It may be a word of knowledge or wisdom or a prophetic action (something we must *do*), but obeying the *rhema* of God's Word will allow His victory to be accomplished through us. Just as He did for Jehoshaphat, God speaks a *now* word that will break through the enemy's plans. When the Israelites were backed up against the Red Sea, Moses told the people to *"stand still, and see the salvation of the Lord"* (Exod. 14:13a). Moses had the M.O.: as a prophetic action, he stretched his rod over the sea, and God destroyed the entire Egyptian army. When Paul and Silas were flogged, jailed, and slated for death, they couldn't use their own abilities to fight to get out. Instead they praised and God fought. He sent an earthquake that not only freed them, but also led the jailer to repent (see Acts 16:22-40). When Peter escaped from prison, God's M.O. was to send an angel (see Acts 12:4-11). All these people faced horrific battles, but they chose to give the battle to God; they praised Him, obeyed, and knew that, through Him, victory was assured.

POWER

Satan wars against us to get that victorious Word out of us and test our faith in God's ability. That Word is both the *logos*, Scriptures we can hold onto, and the *rhema*, that which God has spoken to us as a current promise. Matthew 13:3-8 tells how a sower planted seed. Some fell by the wayside, and birds ate it; some without depth withered in the sun; some were choked by thorns; but some fell in good earth and yielded a great crop. As Christians, we need to let our seed grow in good, fertile soil. Satan's intention, however, is to sidetrack us to keep us from stepping into God's promise and provision that assures victory. Matthew 13:21b says, *"When tribulation or persecution ariseth because of the word, by and by he is offended,"* and that's when he comes after us. Despite what circumstances look like, if we go confidently into battle armed with a *rhema* that tells us the outcome, we'll be victorious and make choices that will positively impact that battle. Therefore, we should *"take the helmet of salvation, and the sword of the Spirit, which is the word [rhema] of God"* (Eph. 6:17). That *rhema* is our unbeatable weapon.

Remember, we learned in the Water Gate that God *"give[s us] power [exousia] to tread on serpents and scorpions, and over all the power [dunamis] of the enemy: and nothing shall by any means hurt"* us (Luke 10:19). Our *exousia* is more powerful than the enemy's *dunamis*. That's our promise despite the fact that our *"adversary the devil, as a roaring lion, walketh about, seeking whom he may devour"* (1 Pet. 5:8). I once saw a vision of satan walking around, scary and roaring. However, when he bellowed, I saw he was toothless. Through God, satan has *no* power over us despite his rantings because Jesus said NOTHING can hurt us. Triumph is assured since we understand we're fighting by Christ's victory on Calvary and can *"resist the devil, and he will flee"* from us (James 4:7b). Now that we know who we are in Holy Spirit and are growing in the Word, we're perpetual overcomers.

FAITH

So how can we do warfare with satan? Often, when we want a victory, we try to do so with whatever our carnal mind can fathom: fists, counselors, weapons, nicotine patches, restraining orders, therapy, or a myriad of other things. We must realize a Christian's battles are spiritual, and *"we do not war after the flesh: (for the weapons of our warfare are not carnal, but mighty through God to the pulling down of strong holds)"* (2 Cor. 10:3b-4). It's not business as usual when we choose spiritual weapons or identify an adversary because we often mistakenly think our battle is against a person afflicting us. But *"we wrestle not against flesh and blood, but against principalities, against powers, against the rulers of the darkness of this world, against spiritual wickedness in high places"* (Eph. 6:12). So, our weapons and our enemy cannot be seen with the natural eye. We war against the devil who doesn't want us to find the M.O. that will activate our faith to believe God is in control.

Second Corinthians 3 says the key to victory is entering into Christ's finished work. Hebrews 4:11a tells us to *"labour therefore to enter into* [His] *rest."* This paradoxical Scripture tells us that the laboring we do isn't to fight satan with our own arsenal, but rather to win the mental battle to enter His rest—so we don't have to lose sleep, develop ulcers, get wrinkles, or have any other worry results. Through prayers, fasting, travail, or any Holy Spirit tool, we break through until we find a *rhema* we can stand on. Then we enter into His rest because, whether we see results yet or not, it's done. Often, after the *rhema* comes, God will give instructions, His personal M.O. to us, for what we're to do. We just obey and let God do the rest.

Romans 10:17 tells us that faith is the result of having heard and believed a *rhema*, which gives direction and victory. When God spoke to

David, Gideon, Jehoshaphat, and others, He understood exactly how to make their victories come about, so He revealed His plan and awaited their obedience. I've seen that often in other situations. Once a man wanted to assume a leadership role in a church I attended, but his doctrine didn't align with the Word. Since he was good at hiding his faulty beliefs, many were deceived. Though it seemed he'd won the battle, as our meeting to vote on him began, God gave me one simple question to ask him. His defensive, belligerent response made people see his heart, and suddenly what had been hidden before was revealed. Members immediately rejected him for leadership, and God achieved victory. Each time we receive that M.O. that produces the *rhema* for us, our faith grows. This allows us to walk confidently in victory, triumphing and being more than a conqueror. No matter through whom our battle comes—even if it's in our own minds—our victory is from God, and satan is defeated.

One morning we were driving to church when my friend Linda came to my mind. I saw her in a vision, discouraged and confused. When we got to church, the service led into ministry, so I told Linda I felt led for our pastor to pray for her about what I'd seen. I didn't know that earlier that morning, God had spoken to the pastor that He was going to give breakthrough to people. He told the pastor to do a prophetic action: blow up a balloon slowly and that breakthrough would come when the balloon burst. As he blew, Linda's and others' expectancy grew. He spoke the words God had given until finally when the balloon popped, all over the congregation, people were slain in the Spirit. Holy Spirit rushed on Linda like a flood, and she could barely stand up. She soaked in this presence for a long time, and God truly did a work. By Tuesday when she came to prayer meeting, she said her life had changed. Those things she'd been battling had lifted, and peace had settled in. Because God gave a *rhema* both to our pastor and me, obedience brought results into fruition.

When God gives His M.O., our part is to do what He says. It may be to march seven times around the city (see Josh. 6:15-21). It may be to dip in a dirty river (see 2 Kings 5:14). It may be to take pitchers and lamps into a battle (see Judg. 7:16-22) or to listen until the enemy's marching comes in the tops of the mulberry trees (see 2 Sam. 5:23-25). It may be to spit in some dirt and put it on blind eyes (see John 9:6-7) or to lay hands on an Arizona woman dying with cancer. It may be to ask a question at a church meeting. Or just to pop a balloon. God knows exactly what battle plan will win, and with Him, foolish things often bring results. Like Jesus, Jehoshaphat, Moses, David, Peter, Paul, and Silas, once we can come to the place of rest, the battle is won, though results may not yet be manifested. We horses just must trust and obey Him exactly as we did in the Sheep Gate.

TOOLS

At this gate we can use tools with which God has empowered us. Many battles can be avoided entirely because God lets His people know in advance, they go to prayer and find a *rhema*, and they get victory before the conflict occurs. Time and again God has given revelation that changed the direction of Christians' lives. Once my sister Suzy dreamt her daughter Wendi died three times. During the dream she also sensed a distinct, evil feeling. As weird as that dream seemed, she knew God was warning her. Within a few days, she had that same feeling, and each time told Wendi to move away from where she was. Then, she saw the Lord's hand: when metal debris was thrown from a lawnmower into the wall where Wendi had been sitting, when the iron dropped and stuck into the floor where Wendi had been lying, and when the swing set collapsed and fell where Wendi had been. Satan doesn't play fair; he goes after us, and our kids, any way he can. But with tools God has given us, we're armed, ready, and victorious.

We can win the battle because we know it's God's. He paid for triumph by His Son's life. Power exists because we know Whom we serve, what rights He's given us as His children, and that the battle is not ours but His. No matter how strong we are in God, He's the victor. It's won *"not by might, nor by power, but by My spirit, saith the Lord of hosts"* (Zech. 4:6b). We're strong horses, but true might comes from Him. The Word shows, through people like David's 400 or Gideon's 300, that the battle belongs to the Lord, not necessarily to the strongest army. Victory doesn't belong to a ruling political party, an unfair employer, a prosecutor, or a wealthy opponent, and it certainly doesn't belong to satan. It's secured because we're found in Christ. Therefore, when we need direction and peace, we don't have to battle; just believe, obey, and *"let God arise,* [and] *let His enemies be scattered"* (Ps. 68:1a).

CONCLUSION

Battles come in all shapes and sizes and from many directions. Perhaps it's a contrary coworker. A philandering spouse. A serious illness. An addicted child. A depleted bank account. An unfair legal system. As we add to the list, we can see each as a battle plaguing us, but we don't always recognize who the author of the battle is. We aren't fighting against a boss, a husband, a child, a paycheck, or a judge. Our enemy is satan, who manipulates and controls situations until we think no hope exists. Our victory doesn't come, though, as John Wayne rides into the picture on his beautiful stallion. It doesn't come by our words or worries. God doesn't need us to fret and figure until our minds are spent. Victory comes by finding His will, trusting His *rhema,* and obeying. The way God works it all out is perfect, His timing is right, and His victory is complete. There's a way to overcome, and His name is wonderful Father.

In Acts 20, Paul recounts to the elders at Ephesus some of the battles he's fought. He's endured many hardships—but then he says, *"None of these things move me, neither count I my life dear unto myself, so that I might finish my course with joy..."* (Acts 20:24). After a battle *"your sorrow shall be turned into joy"* (John 16:20), a fruit of the Spirit. John goes on to say that during labor, a woman has pain that she forgets after the birth (see John 16:21). Sometimes battles require travail that produces a birth of God's promises, and that brings joy that far surpasses the preceding battle. At this gate, we must learn to take authority over the enemy, find God's M.O. for the skirmish, give that battle to our Lord, and press on into our blood-bought victory. We must learn to pray the Word and know our authority through that Word, Jesus' name, and Holy Spirit's power. We must find His rhema, obey, and then stand on it. We're strong when we're weak enough to lean on Him. Hmm. Seems like we started learning that lesson a long time ago!

9

The East Gate: Fostering Worship

After them repaired Zadok the son of Immer over against his house. After him repaired also Shemaiah the son of Shechaniah, the keeper of the east gate (Nehemiah 3:29).

My children are now grown, and every moment of being a mom, even the difficult ones, resonated with me. When they were teens, I embarrassed them with anything I did, but it didn't start out that way. When they were young, I was the center of their world. They wanted to dress like me (they still cringe about an Orlando Spring Break trip when we all wore matching bathing suits). They wanted to go with me everywhere and do whatever I did. When we watched television, they both wanted to sit by me. One morning, I remember surveying my reflection in the mirror when I was getting dressed. I had gained about 30 pounds, and I looked terrible.

"Man, I have to lose weight," I said disgustedly. "I'm so fat."

Jennifer had come into the bedroom and heard my last words. "Are you fat, Mommy?" she asked incredulously. She was probably around two and understood the concept of *fat,* but since she knew it was negative, she couldn't imagine how that could apply to me. Jennifer saw all my fat and moles and lumps and bad hair days, but she knew nothing but perfection in me because she loved me so much.

The Lord longs for the same adoration from us. He wants us to be exactly like our young children who sat on our laps just to be near us. This devotion and fostering of worship for the Lord is an amazing part of our journey with Him. When we learn to worship, our lives will be forever changed because He'll show up to be with us. He longs for us to love Him and desire to be in His presence. He wants us to crawl into His lap and say simply, "I love You, Father." Too often our communication with Him is only when we want something. He longs for us to be His children who desire to be with Him, just because and not like some self-serving teen who says he loves us because he wants the car keys. He craves the praise and worship He deserves, *just because.*

THE EAST GATE

As I began studying the gates, I arrived at the last two. Along the way, I'd learned a lot that clarified phases of my Christian walk. Then I came to the East Gate and began to research. As I read, a consensus existed among most scholars that the East Gate represented the return of Christ. The East Gate faces the Mount of Olives and has been kept closed in anticipation of the Messiah's coming. I look forward to that event and believe our generation will see it. I felt, however, there had to be another message for us in our Christian walk. Every other gate has had an application for our lives in Christ *today,* not only for a coming event. His return is in the future even if it's five minutes away. As I reflected on this, I sought the Lord. He impressed me that the importance of this gate for our "now" walk is that it represents our worship. This very important aspect of our relationship creates intimacy with God and maturity in us, yet is a facet many Christians fail to step into.

During Nehemiah's time, the East Gate was probably the temple's eastern gate. Our bodies, too, are the temple of the Lord, and we must *"present* [them as] *a living sacrifice, holy, acceptable unto God, which is* [our] *reasonable service"* (Rom. 12:1b). This Scripture has been important in several of the gates, for we must constantly consider sacrifice. It takes on a new meaning, however, in the East Gate. The Greek word here for *service* is *latreia,* which means "ministration of God, i.e. worship."[1] The same word describes Jewish worship ceremonies in the temple (see Heb. 9:1,6). We must serve with worship: what an awesome revelation! In this context, the word *reasonable, logikos,* means "rational."[2] Considering Who He is and all He's done, is doing, and will do for us, our unreserved, unending worship should be natural. It's what we've been created to do.

The keeper of gate who made repairs was *Shemaiah,* which means one "that hears or obeys the Lord."[3] Through worship, we accomplish both. We hear Him as a result of worship, and by the act of worship, we obey His command. Worship is a building block of our relationship with Him, so it's incumbent on us to come to Him regularly. Shemaiah is the son of *Shechaniah,* which means "habitation of the Lord."[4] Psalm 22:3 says, *"Thou art holy, O Thou that inhabitest the praises of Israel."* In other words, God dwells where we praise and worship. My mom always said that you never really know someone until you have lived with him or her. Because I've lived with my children and husband, we know each other's personalities, good and bad. When something bothers any of us, we sense it immediately because intimacy comes through spending time together. The same goes for God. When we worship, we get into His presence and understand His mind. He lives in us, for we are His habitation. For those who want intimacy, worship is the key.

JESUS AS MESSIAH

To appreciate fully the East Gate, we must first realize a concept basic to the gate—Jesus is Messiah. In Luke, Jesus is in the temple and reads from the Book of Isaiah:

> *The Spirit of the Lord is upon Me, because He hath anointed Me to preach the gospel to the poor; He hath sent Me to heal the brokenhearted, to preach deliverance to the captives, and recovering of sight to the blind, to set at liberty them that are bruised, to preach the acceptable year of the Lord. And He closed the book, and He gave it again to the minister, and sat down. And the eyes of all them that were in the synagogue were fastened on Him. And He began to say unto them, This*

day is this scripture fulfilled in your ears" (Luke 4:18-21; from Isaiah 61:1).

This Scripture may not mean much to us except that Jesus was declaring His sovereignty. However, Hebrews would have understood that the Scripture was fulfilled before their eyes. It proclaimed the Messiah's coming, and by His actions Jesus declared Himself to be the awaited one. They would have realized by Jewish tradition that Jesus punctuated Isaiah's prophecy when He sat in a chair reserved for the Messiah. Luke said, *"The eyes of all them that were in the synagogue were fastened on Him"* because they were amazed at the man who had just sat in the sacred seat. They would have understood the implication that He, Jesus, was proclaiming Himself as Messiah.

Another event involving the East Gate declared His majesty. Zechariah 9:9 prophesied,

Rejoice greatly, O daughter of Zion; shout, O daughter of Jerusalem: behold, thy King cometh unto thee: He is just, and having salvation; lowly, and riding upon an ass, and upon a colt the foal of an ass.

In Matthew 21:1-2, Mark 11:1-3, and Luke 19:29-31, this prophecy comes to fruition:

When they drew nigh unto Jerusalem, and were come to Beth-phage, unto the mount of Olives, then sent Jesus two disciples, saying unto them, Go into the village over against you, and straightway ye shall find an ass tied, and a colt with her: loose them, and bring them unto Me (Matthew 21:1-2).

Jesus' disciples got a donkey in Bethphage on the east slope of the Mount of Olives; Bethany was on the southeast side of the Mount, two miles east of Jerusalem (see John 11:18). Because the places mentioned in the story of Jesus' triumphal entry into Jerusalem were near that gate, more than likely Jesus used the East Gate as He entered into Jerusalem on the donkey.

This fulfills the prophecy in Ezekiel 44:1-2:

Then He brought me back the way of the gate of the outward sanctuary which looketh toward the east; and it was shut. Then said the Lord unto me; This gate shall be shut, it shall not be opened, and no man shall enter in by it; because the Lord, the God of Israel, hath entered in by it....

Even though the Bible doesn't say specifically Jesus used the East Gate, the implication is that He did. Jews would know that particular tradition and would understand that by coming through this gate, Jesus was declaring Himself as Messiah. He entered into Jerusalem on Palm Sunday with throngs cheering Him. That sounds like worship. Luke 19:37-38 says,

When He was...at the descent of the mount of Olives, the whole multitude of the disciples began to rejoice and praise God with a loud voice for all the mighty works that they had seen; saying, Blessed be the King that cometh in the name of the Lord: peace in heaven, and glory in the highest!

The majesty associated with His entrance was befitting the king whose coming had been prophesied. Zechariah 14:4 also said He would stand on the Mount of Olives in the east. Much evidence proved He was truly the Messiah.

Even His birth related to the east. In Matthew 2, wise men, who came from the east, saw His star in the east and followed it as it moved toward where baby Jesus was. Just as the eastern star declared His birth, so will the east proclaim His coming return (see Matt. 2:1-2,9). Matthew 24:27 says, *"For as the lightning cometh out of the east, and shineth even unto the west; so shall also the coming of the Son of man be."* Anticipation of the Messiah's return is still prevalent in Jerusalem where people believe that, when He comes in glory and splendor, He'll reenter the city through this East Gate. A Muslim cemetery is now in front of the East Gate. Muslims also believe Bible prophecy will be fulfilled; to prevent Messiah from entering by this gate, they sealed the gate during the sixteenth century. While trying to thwart His return, they instead fulfilled the Ezekiel 44 prophecy by not allowing access through the gate.[5] Truly, Jesus is the Messiah that was and is predicted to come through the East Gate.

So, Jesus is truly the Messiah—but how does He relate to worship? He's what our walk is all about. He so longs for our worship that when *"the whole multitude of the disciples"* exalted Him, *"saying, Blessed be the King that cometh in the name of the Lord: peace in heaven, and glory in the highest"* (Luke 19:37-38), He responded to criticism coming from the Pharisees in this way: *"If these should hold their peace, the stones would immediately cry out"* (Luke 19:40b). All creation was made to worship, so we're also to lift up Him and the Father. Do you remember when your kids were young, they looked into your eyes, and said, "I love you, Mommy / Daddy"? Your heart was filled with joy to hear that proclamation. God desires for us just to love and worship Him, our Abba, our Daddy. He wants us to come to Him—not with an agenda, but only to love Him. He wants us to approach Him with our hands up, not out.

PRAISE

Judah, which means "praise of the Lord," represents praise and worship.[6] While the children travelled through the wilderness, Judah was positioned east and went first before other tribes. Hosea 10:11c says, *"Judah shall plow, and Jacob shall break his clods."* Praise (Judah) makes the ground able to be sown for salvation, breakthrough, and deliverance. Numbers 2:9 says, *"All that were numbered in the camp of Judah....These shall first set forth."* Praise must go first as we make our own wilderness journey. Genesis 49:8-10 affirms that Judah will be on the *"neck"* of the enemy and will receive honor from others. Praise is the backbone of everything else; before we go to battle, praise needs to precede us. Remember when Jehoshaphat won the battle because the worshipers went first? Praise was the tool God used then and still uses now to bring us to a place of victory.

The story of Joseph teaches about praise. Genesis 37 tells of Joseph being sold into slavery by his brothers. Genesis 39 records the story of Joseph's service to Potiphar and his time in prison. The chapter that comes in between, Genesis 38, tells the sordid story of Judah and Tamar, his daughter-in-law whose husband had died. Judah hadn't fulfilled his duty to make sure Tamar had someone with whom to bear a child, so she disguised herself and lay with Judah. She became pregnant by him and gave birth to twins, Perez and Zerah. The positioning of this story is interesting because it seems to have little to do with Joseph and how God prepared him to rule in Egypt. I believe the meanings of the names of these characters holds a key: *Joseph* means "increase; addition"; *Judah,* "praise of the Lord"; *Tamar,* "palm tree [peace, oasis]"; *Perez,* "divided [breakthrough]"; and *Zerah,* "brightness [revelation]."[7] When *praise* combines with *peace,* it brings *breakthrough,* which precedes *revelation.* This, then, brings *abundance,* which Joseph later experienced. During this time in Joseph's life, it didn't seem like he had plenty, but God was setting it up. How often do we want to break through a barrier in our lives but just can't seem to do it? Praise and worship bring that breakthrough.

FIRST REFERENCE

The first reference to the east occurs in a passage in Genesis 2:10-14. A river that watered Eden went from the Garden, and then split into four tributaries. Those four parts of the river correspond to things that have often accompanied times I've experienced intense worship. *Pison* (changing) is in the land of *Havilah* (that suffers pain, that brings forth), which has gold (divinity), bdellium (a fragrant, amber resin or pearl), and onyx (a gem of pale, green color). The second river was *Gihon* (valley of grace) in *Cush* (blackness); the third was *Hiddekel* (a sharp voice, a sound), which goes *east* of *Assyria* (same as Ashur, "who is happy"); and the fourth was *Euphrates* (that makes fruitful).[8] The Holy Spirit river that waters is what I experience while I'm worshiping: I come away refreshed from that time.

As the rivers split into different ways, their descriptions correspond to what that refreshing water of worship does. First, it changes our lives and things in us (Pison). One of God's great paradoxes is that when we're down, we can put on *"the garment of praise for the spirit of heaviness"* (Isa. 61:3), and worship changes our perspective. It often takes us into an intense place of intercession and travail, the level which, like childbirth, births amazing breakthroughs (Havilah). Through worship, prayers are answered, for *"if any man be a worshipper of God, and doeth His will, him He heareth"* (John 9:31), and those are the treasures and precious gems that are found in that land (gold, bedellium, and onyx). God's grace (Gihon) coupled with His voice (Hiddekel) brings happiness (Assyria) and fruitfulness (Euphrates) even in darkness (Ethiopia). Those are amazing by products that come as a result of sincere, no-agenda worship.

One night we were having Bible Study in our home. Wade had finished with his teaching, and we had begun to worship. That group had gone many times into His presence, but that night we worshipped with an amazing intensity. Two women who were sitting side by side on the couch were instantly healed from things that had been plaguing them. Another time, when Wade and I were worshipping alone, a presence stronger than I had rarely felt came into the room. As we worshipped, it seemed we could feel that presence saturate our beings as minutes stretched into nearly two hours. As a result of our spending time in His presence, a dire need we'd had for a while was answered the next day, and we had clarity regarding a decision we'd been praying about. God's treasures (often those gems literally fall from Heaven in different places in the world) are there for us, and worship is the conduit for Him to heap them on.

The tributary in Eden that relates to this gate's purpose most, though, is *Hiddekel,* which goes east and means "a sharp voice, a sound."[9] Whenever I hear a biblical description of a powerful voice, I think of how God's voice has been linked with many strong descriptions. David called it *"mighty"* (Psalm 68:33), *"powerful...[and] full of majesty"* (Psalm 29:4). He says God's voice is so mighty that it *"breaketh the cedars"* (Psalm. 29:5), *"divideth the flames"* (Psalm 29:7), *"shaketh the wilderness"* (Psalm 29:8), *"makes the deer give birth"* (Psalm 29:9 NKJV), and could "melt" the earth (see Psalm 46:6). Job says God *"thundereth marvellously with His voice"* (Job 37:5) and described the *"rumbling that comes from His mouth"* (Job 37:2 NKJV) and *"voice of his excellency*" (Job 37:4). John described His voice as *"loud"* (Rev. 12:10), a *"trumpet"* (Rev. 1:10), and *"great thunder"* (Rev. 14:2). Paul said God's voice *"shook the earth"* (Heb. 12:26). Ezekiel includes God's speaking with a list of overwhelmingly loud things: — *"the noise of many waters"* and *"a tumult like the noise of an army"* (Ezek. 1:24 NKJV). I think of this comparison to great waters like when you stand in front of Niagara Falls with the sound so deafening you can barely hear; it's *"a noise of many waters"* (Ezekiel. 43:2) or a *"voice as the sound of many waters"* (Rev. 1:15). Those references give an inkling of the magnitude of the voice of our Father.

So why would the unimaginably powerful sound of God's voice be connected with the East Gate? His intimidating voice and authority are our advocate against our enemies. Isaiah 30:30-32 says that when we worship, the Lord goes to battle for us. He will...

> *...cause His glorious voice to be heard, and shall shew the lighting down of His arm...with the flame of a devouring fire, with scattering, and tempest, and hailstones. For through the voice of the Lord shall the Assyrian be beaten down...with tabrets [tambourines] and harps: and in battles of shaking will He fight with it.*

In other words, the Lord beats our enemies soundly in conjunction with praise and worship. The Amplified Bible says, *"He attacks [Assyria] with swinging and menacing arms"* (Isa. 30:32). God is going to fight whatever battles come along. When we worship, though, we open the door for Him to do that with the intensity of a *"devouring fire"* and *"swinging and menacing arms."* How do you think the enemy will respond to that?

WORSHIP'S FACE

Worship makes our prayer life fertile. A few years ago, the Lord led me to intercede for a young man who was being tempted into a promiscuous lifestyle. Each morning as I did my devotions, I worshiped. One day, the anointing was stronger and more intense than usual, and I could sense a strong presence of angels. While in that atmosphere, I felt led to dispatch angels to various assignments. One was for this young man. That morning, as I indicated where I wanted them to go, I could feel the hair on the side of my face move as they went to do the bidding of the Word of God. Worship opened the door for me to receive the fullness of what God had. It wasn't long until news came that this young man had turned his life around. Praise and worship created the atmosphere for God to send Heaven's resources to battle *"with swinging and menacing arms"* on behalf of that young man.

Worship is crucial to the growth of a Christian, but most Christians don't worship. Wade and I travel to many churches, and though most praise teams perform pretty music with talented musicians, most of them don't understand worship. It's treated as a performance for the congregation, but that's way off the mark. True worship is raising the name of Jesus to exalt His wondrous character. I once heard someone describe worship as performing for an audience of one—our Lord. Psalm 29:2 says, *"Give unto the Lord the glory due unto His name; worship the Lord in the beauty of holiness."*

Remember, *Shemaiah* (who hears or obeys the Lord), son of *Shechaniah* (habitation of the Lord) made repairs on this gate. We obey God when we worship Him, and worship is where God dwells. Jeremiah 7:2 says,

> *Stand in the gate of the Lord's house, and proclaim there this word, and say, Hear the word of the Lord, all ye of Judah, that enter in at these gates to worship the Lord.*

The word of the Lord that comes at this gate is to worship, which is our purpose and priority. Isaiah 27:13 says all will *"worship the Lord in the holy mount at Jerusalem."* This gate is both literally and figuratively the Holy Mount—where we should spend a great portion of our devotional time.

We can truly worship after our Fountain Gate experience because real worship is part of Holy Spirit's work in us. In John 4:23-24, the Greek word rendered "spirit" is *pneuma*, often translated as Holy Spirit. Here, Jesus says,

*The hour cometh, and now is, when the true worshipers shall worship the Father in spirit and in truth: for the Father seeketh such to worship Him. God is a Spirit: and they that worship Him must worship **Him in spirit** and in truth.*

I think it's interesting that the verse describes how "true worshipers" will worship: The four uses of *worship* are *proskuneo* "to kiss, like a dog licking his master's hand..., prostrate oneself in homage (do reverence to, adore), worship."[10] Our "true" worship isn't a half-hearted effort but rather should be total abandonment and adoration of the Father. How sad that even churches where Holy Spirit operates neglect this crucial aspect of our walk. God doesn't just *suggest* we worship Him; He *requires* all creation to worship. After we understand its importance, we should to get to a place of radical worship. Just as David made a fool of himself as he worshipped God while bringing the ark back to Jerusalem, we should be fools for Him and lift His name high—loudly and proudly.

THE GLORY

That radical worship brings anointing, which ushers in the glory of God. *Shekinah* (glory) came into the Temple from/through the Eastern Gate. Ezekiel 43:4 says, *"And the glory of the Lord came into the house by the way of the gate* [which looks toward] *the east."* Glory, God's presence in our midst, came in through this East Gate of Jerusalem; we usher in His glory by worship as we die to ourselves and lift Him higher. The more we worship, the more we're in His presence. Worship is the key. We look into Jesus' face, we climb into Father's lap, and worship brings glory. Ezekiel 10:19b says, *"Every one stood at the door of the east gate of the Lord's house; and the glory of the God of Israel was over them above."* Standing in this gate takes us into the glory because the door is opened by our worship. Glory brings peace and often, like Perez and Zerah, breakthrough and revelation. God has revealed His secrets many times to Wade and me as a result of worshipping to the glory. As we become more accustomed to a lifestyle of worship, we can traverse through different places where God can show Himself.

Each place promotes intimacy with Him, gives us something we need to go on, and takes us deeper in Him. Most of us never cross into the glory because we don't even make it into the first part—worship. When Wade and I worship at home or with others during Bible Studies, it usually goes into glory and feels like a heavy blanket on us. The glory manifests in a variety of ways—a cloud of fog or mist fills the room, an intense peace arrives, or people can't move their limbs. Sometimes worshippers become slain in the Spirit and lie immobile for hours. Once as I was sitting at the piano soaking in His presence, I couldn't hold my head up, and it dropped onto the keys. I sat like that until I could move again. During our meetings, some people have gone out in the Spirit and been taken into a deep revelatory trance. In other places around the world, manna and jewels have dropped from Heaven. God is giving miracles, providing deliverances, and raising people from the dead. Each of these manifestations is God's way of sending us a message—"I long to dwell in your worship. Here's a kiss for you from Me."

We became used to gold dust falling during our meetings. Then one week in Bible Study, a lady received a gold tooth filling shaped like a cross. We'd read about and seen videos telling of such occurrences, but this was the first time any of us had witnessed it, and we were all very excited to see it in person. About a week after that, as Wade was brushing his teeth one night, he saw something glint in his mouth. When he looked, he had a new gold tooth on the right. On the left, gold fillings and a gold bracket on one tooth shone brightly. We were dumbfounded at God's might and spent the next few days trying to wrap our minds around the possibilities this event spoke to us. That night, our lives were forever changed. We went into a deeper realm with the Father who said, "If I can give you a gold tooth, can't I do other miraculous things you haven't even begun to imagine?" Since that time, we've seen an intensity in our meetings and others', too. God is letting us know He's still on His throne and still wants our attention.

These wonders, however, have been met with mixed reactions, mostly skepticism. Wade and I know *these signs shall follow them that believe* that God can do anything, so His little nuggets follow us around because of our belief (Mark 16:17). If you remember, back in the Fish Gate we said many things will bring in unbelievers. God's manifestations of love are sent because He knows what will touch every one of us, from hardcore, cynical Christians, to hardcore, unbelieving sinners. Whether people believe in how God manifests or not isn't our concern. It's God's, and He knows how to reach us all. He can do anything He wants for anybody and doesn't need our help to decide what will touch each of us. Our job is to receive His gifts and cherish them. Joseph knew his brothers were jealous of that multi-colored coat, but he wore it regardless of their envy because it was his father's special gift to him. Wade wears his dental work and shows it frequently because it was *his* Father's special gift to him. These amazing manifestations aren't what this gate is about, however. They're just an added bonus. The real purpose of the East Gate is all about His presence, and that's what we must become addicted to.

CONCLUSION

I love a story my friend Sharon tells. Her son was in Bible college in Pensacola during the River Movement. After worship, the glory came in and filled the room with God's powerful presence. She thought it was weird because people were not only lying on the floor but were also glued to the walls. Then, the unthinkable happened—she somehow got stuck like Velcro on a nearby wall, too. She had all her faculties but just couldn't move. She whispered for her son, "Matt...Matt...Matthew," but he never came to help her down. Later, when she was able to move, she sat beside him.

"Why didn't you get me down?" she asked.

"They told us when people are stuck on the walls to just leave 'em there." Apparently, this was a place that had become intimately acquainted with how God's glory operates. It's not what we might choose, but when God is in control, we do it His oh-so-glorious way. What a tremendous thing to know He's given us just a taste of what worship can bring us into.

The East Gate is where Jesus came into Jerusalem and will again, once more declaring that He is Messiah. We, too, must travel through the East Gate to create relationship with Him and Almighty God, who long to live in our praises. He yearns for intimacy that comes through worship. In exchange for our worship, He gives so much more than we can imagine. Ezekiel 11:1 says,

> *The spirit lifted me up, and brought me unto the east gate of the Lord's house...I saw Jaazaniah* [whom the Lord will hear] *the son of Azur* [he that assists or is assisted], *and Pelatiah* [a deliverance of the Lord] *the son of Benaiah* [son of the Lord], *princes of the people.*[11]

Worship promises all those things: the Lord hears, assists, delivers, and takes us into His family. Christians who don't worship are missing much of the glorious depth that comes as we walk through our own gates toward the final one—our assignment.

CHAPTER 10

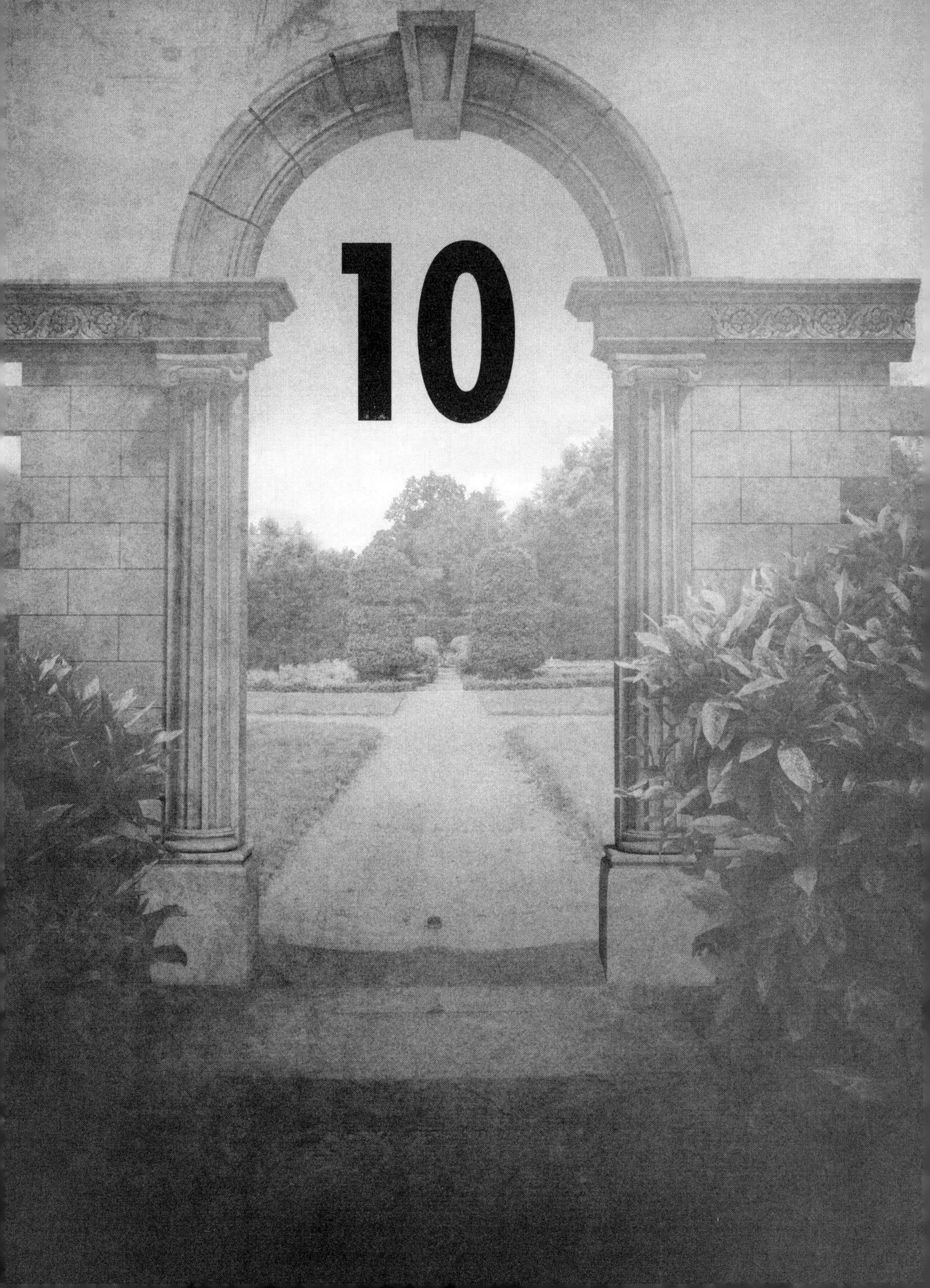

The Gate Miphkad: Fulfilling Our Destiny

After him repaired Malchiah the goldsmith's son unto the place of the Nethinims, and of the merchants, over against the gate Miphkad, and to the going up of the corner (Nehemiah 3:31).

Every year of my young life, I trudged through a necessary evil that seemed interminable but ultimately paid off—education. While I was going through every phase, I couldn't understand what its purpose was, but each prepared me for the next and led to the ultimate reason for my education—going into a career. Starting in kindergarten, I learned basics and social skills (which I mastered a little too well) that would serve me later. As simple as those proficiencies seem to a high schooler, if an elementary student misses basics along the way, he's often handicapped for the rest of his life. As I progressed through junior high, high school, and college, I saw how teachers, classes, books, and friends had a role in bringing me into the fulfillment of my goals.

As a former high school composition teacher, I know firsthand that students often don't see how education prepares them for their lives. When they came to me as juniors, some had neglected to learn what they needed to be successful in my class. They struggled until they caught up with what they should know. Some also didn't see that, although they didn't like English, what they were learning prepared them for where they would go after they left my classroom. They had such a narrow vision that they didn't see how writing skills would be crucial for college and career, so some never progressed. Those were the ones who went to the university unprepared. Students who went to college with well-developed writing skills could concentrate on classes that would prepare them in their chosen career.

This reminds me of our Christian evolution. We may not grasp the purpose in many phases or gates we go through until we're finished with them, but God sees the bigger picture. He has the end result in mind when He teaches us each skill. If we skip lessons or adopt a mistrustful attitude, He can't send us on until we learn to submit to His wisdom. He knows what we require to get to where we need ultimately to be. From the beginning He's had plans for us, so He schools us before we can graduate and go to a higher level. We must be lifelong learners—even when we're finally in the place of our destiny.

THE GATE OF MIPHKAD

This last gate, the one for which this journey was developed, takes us into the place God designed just for us. When I first began this study, nearly everything I read spoke of how this gate represents final judgment. As Christians, we always must be aware that our earthly journey is going to end with judgment. But just as at the East Gate, I asked, "Lord, what about now? How does this gate affect my walk with You today?" The Lord spoke into my spirit and said this is the gate where we receive our assignment from Him. The Hebrew word *miphkad* means "an appointment, i.e. mandate, a designated spot, appointed place...assignment."[1] We've gone through training to end up with whatever assignment God has for us. This gate was in the northeast wall near the Sheep Gate, so now our journey has come full circle back to the place where we entered. All that we endured has prepared us for this gate. What has God been growing us up to do? Here we can understand it's not just *what* we are—a pastor, teacher, evangelist, missionary—but *who* we are—a child of the King bought and paid for by Christ back at the Sheep Gate. Whatever assignment God has for us, He's the One who does it through us.

Malchijah (the Lord my king or my counselor), a goldsmith, repaired to the house of the temple servants, the Nethinim (given or offered).[2] If the Lord our King directs our lives and we offer ourselves as that sacrifice we've learned about throughout the gates, we'll come into our destinies. During the gates' progression, God has been like a goldsmith, who purifies gold and lets dross come to the top so the gold is refined and precious. Even though we're now in the Assignment Gate, that refining is still taking place. The Nethinim, like us, offered themselves to be used by God, and we, too, are servants in our assignment. In the Bible, this gate is mentioned only in this single Scripture. Our Gate of Miphkad, our assignment, is created just for us because we are...

> ...*fearfully and wonderfully made....*[Our] *substance was not hid from* [God], *when* [we were] *made in secret....*[His] *eyes did see* [our] *substance, yet being unperfect; and in* [His] *book all* [our] *members were written...when as yet there was none of them* (Psalm 139:14-16).

Before we were born or even conceived, before we had the potential that God, our parents, our education, and our intelligence gave us, He saw our substance. Just as a potter has a plan when she starts to make her creation, so our Creator has a plan for us. This gate is why we made our journey through all the other gates.

JUDGMENT

As much as the world wants to ignore it, Heaven and hell are realities. Many come through the Sheep Gate to escape a fiery eternity but find much more in this Christianity thing than just saying the words and holding on till they die. At the end of our human journey on Earth, God will call all souls for judgment. Hebrews 9:27 says, *"It is appointed unto men once to die, but after this the judgment."* When we came into the Sheep Gate, we learned that reality. God called us to a Christian life, and we're ecstatic to know that at the end we'll get our eternal reward. Judgment is real, and, as Paul says, *"It is a fearful thing to fall into the hands of the living God"* (Heb. 10:31).

Judgment for Christians, though, is not about Heaven and hell, for we made that decision when we came into the family of God. Our judgment is how we're to be rewarded. One day all of us will be judged about what we did on Earth. Paul says someday all of us will *"appear before the judgment seat of Christ; that every one may receive the things done in his body, according to that he hath done, whether it be good or bad"* (2 Cor. 5:10). In his vision John saw a great white throne where the dead were judged for what was written in God's book (see Rev. 20:11-12). As we go through life, even important things we do like working out for better health pale in comparison to our being right with God, *"for bodily exercise profiteth little: but godliness is profitable unto all things, having promise of the life that now is, and of that which is to come"* (1 Tim. 4:8). Judgment is real.

OUR ASSIGNMENT

But what about now? What does this gate represent for me in my walk today? We've been plodding through our journey to get here—the place God's prepared for us. Even though this is the gate where we find our destiny, this isn't the only time God has presented us with assignments. During our journey through the gates, He's prepared us for our Miphkad while building other aspects of our character with jobs along the way. Those assignments determined how faithful we'd be now. Jesus makes that point in the parable of the talents. To one of his servants, the master gave five talents; to another, he gave two; and to the third, he gave one. The first and second servants were diligent about getting other talents, but the third buried his. Because the first two were conscientious, the master said, *"Thou hast been faithful over a few things, I will make thee ruler over many things..."* (Matt. 25:21b). He wants to test our mettle, for whoever *"is faithful in that which is least is faithful also in much"* (Luke 16:10a). God starts us out doing small things to work for Him. When we prove we can handle those, He gives us bigger duties. Those then lead to our Gate of *Miphkad*.

When I was in ninth grade, I started teaching a small children's Sunday school class. It began with three children, but I treated that job as if it were the most important duty in the church. I prepared, kept them busy, taught them, and loved them. It wasn't the biggest job with which I could have been entrusted, but it was important for the operation of the church's ministry. More than that, it taught me to treat little things God gives me as if they're a calling. In the Sheep Gate, we learned Solomon says that whatever we're given, to do it with all we have (see Eccles. 9:10), and that became my Christian mantra. During that time in my journey, not only did I grow and eventually begin other duties of a more seasoned Christian, but before I left the position, so many children attended, the church had to divide the group. Whatever your assignment is at any gate, be faithful, for God is teaching you a lesson that will help you throughout your life.

THE COST

Those experiences, then, prepared us for this gate. What were you saved for—just to go to Heaven and pass the judgment test? Remember when I said some Christians treat salvation like it's only salvation and don't look at what else it can be? The same goes with our Assignment Gate. Are we sold out and want to do the will of God regardless of what it costs?

Paul said, *"I press toward the mark for the prize of the high calling of God in Christ Jesus"* (Phil. 3:14). In Second Corinthians 11, he's addressing issues some of his contemporaries in Corinth had gone through to follow God's call. He said he understood that many of them had suffered much to be *"ministers of Christ,"* but he had suffered *"more; in labours more abundant"* (2 Cor. 11:23). In other words, yes, we all have a cost for our call, but he, who endured more than any of them, still pressed toward the prize. Second Corinthians 11:23-27 lists those things he'd suffered to be in his Gate of *Miphkad:*

- *"stripes above measure"*
- *"in prisons more frequent"*
- *"in deaths oft"*
- *"five times received...forty stripes save* [except] *one"*
- *"thrice...beaten with rods"*

- *"once...stoned"*

- *"thrice...suffered shipwreck"*

- *"a night and a day...in the deep* [sea]*"*

- *"in perils of waters...robbers...* [his own] *countrymen...heathen... in the city...in the wilderness...in the sea...among false brethren; in weariness and painfulness, in watchings* [sleeplessness] *often, in hunger and thirst, in fastings often, in cold and nakedness"*

Once a governor in Damascus even ordered a whole garrison to arrest him, so Paul had to be let down in a basket from a window (see 2 Cor. 11:32-33). Despite all those atrocities that had befallen him, he said he took *"pleasure in infirmities, in reproaches, in necessities, in persecutions, in distresses for Christ's sake: for when I am weak, then am I strong"* (2 Cor. 12:10). Remember that even before Saul became Paul and received his assignment, God told him there would be *"great things he must suffer for* [His] *name's sake"* (Acts 9:16). Ananias' warning didn't dissuade Paul from pursuing the call he received on the Damascus Road to spread the knowledge of Jesus. Still, after all that time and all those hardships, Paul's answer was the same. He could continue on his journey because he'd sold out to the Lord and realized he was nothing outside of Jesus. He could do his *Miphkad* regardless of what came along.

Are we ready for what our Assignment Gate will cost us? Have we counted that cost? Are we willing to give up our own will to do His? Jesus said, *"Many are called, but few are chosen"* (Matt. 22:14), so if we arrived here at the Assignment Gate, it's because we desired more than others or anything to be about the Father's business. I've heard amazing ministers like Benny Hinn say following God's grand plan has often been difficult, but they determined to pursue their destinies with all they have. When my parents were pastors, they often sacrificed a lot of our family time and sometimes their own health to do God's bidding, but they'd also determined to do His call. To go into the gate God has planned for us, we must want that more than anything else in the world. Have we become single-minded about reaching for the *"prize of the high calling"*?

What's your assignment from the Lord? Each of us has a part to fulfill in God's great plan—a destiny—but many factors will determine if we'll be chosen to complete it. Can He trust us, are we sold out, are we willing to count the cost, is our integrity what it should be? Other gates have developed the maturity required to go on to our assignment. Trials, battles, and temptations created who we are now, at this point. We were kneaded and shaped and kneaded and shaped then kneaded and shaped again by the Potter. We learned to please and rely on the Father. We went through everything to come to *Miphkad to* be numbered among those who know who they are, why they're here at this time, and what God will require of them.

In His Time

Once, when we pastored, a young Christian man came to us fretting about what his assignment was from God. We told him the Lord had to do a lot of things in him before that appointment would become a reality in his life. He didn't want to hear that; he longed to plunge into the assignment without God's accomplishing in him whatever needed to happen first. He ultimately lost his zeal to work for God because he didn't become a viable vessel the Potter could use. Just like our natural children's maturation is a process, so along the way, *"let us not be weary in well doing: for in due season we shall reap, if we faint not"* (Gal. 6:9). *Miphkad* reminds us we must overcome and be single-minded about following God. It reminds us that as uncomfortable as some gates are, we progress to this appointed time and purpose by getting rid of unnecessary or harmful things while building a relationship with our Shepherd. It ushers us into our divine assignment, and *"who knoweth whether* [we] *art come to the kingdom for such a time as this?"* (Esther 4:14c).

The call comes to us, but there's always a time period before its implementation comes to fruition. For Moses, after he fled from Egypt to Midian (see Exod. 2:15), he spent 40 years in the desert tending sheep for his father-in-law before his burning bush call (see Exod. 3:10) and his return to Egypt. That wilderness time prepared him for the next 40 years when he would be the leader of God's people in the desert.

After Paul's conversion, he stayed for about three years in Damascus before he went to Jerusalem to begin his ministry. He was there for only two weeks when he had to flee to avoid arrest. He then went to Syria and Cilicia for 14 years before he and Barnabas began their Jerusalem ministry together (see Gal. 1:18–2:1). During that time, he probably made a living as a tent-maker and found ways to be about the Father's business. God has a way of making our experiences weave together to bring us to our place of destiny.

As a boy, Joseph had a dream his brothers would one day bow to him. But before he finally came into the place God had created for him, he was betrayed, sold into slavery, maligned, imprisoned, and forsaken. The journey to his destiny took 13 years for him to be ruling and then 7 more to see his dream about his brothers come to pass. I'm sure at times he wondered if God still saw that outcome that was promised him as he sat day after day in the dank prison where he'd been unjustly sent. But all the tribulations had done a work in him to allow him to rule with godly wisdom and save people of many nations during the famine. David, too, must have wondered if God's plans for him would ever come to fruition. He was a shepherd boy of about 15 when Samuel anointed him, but God knew a lot of work had to be done to prepare him to reign 40 years as Israel's greatest king. He fostered intimacy with God and learned a lesson on worship that served him the rest of his life. He killed a lion and a bear, defeated a giant, calmed evil spirits in Saul, became a great warrior, avoided Saul's murderous intents, and grew in wisdom. He learned how to sink to the bottom and rise to the top again. It took around 17 years for his destiny to come about because God had much to do in him.

Even Jesus didn't come into His purpose overnight. Though He was the Son of God, He still had to go through maturation. He learned a trade, fostered relationships, taught Scripture, and went about the business of preparing for His *Miphkad*. Then He started His ministry at age 30. Our purpose is the same as Jesus'. John 17:18 says, *"As Thou hast sent Me into the world, even so have I also sent them into the world."* John later says that in this world, we're to be just like Jesus (see 1 John 4:17), and conformity to Him is our ultimate goal. What we do is a direct outcome of who we are in Him, and our *Miphkad* will demonstrate His ability. Like all these men, our specific assignment awaits us though that gate seems so far off that at times we think we may never get there and that surely God has forgotten. But we must run with patience and know He's faithful, for He who *"hath begun a good work in* [us] *will perform it..."* (Phil. 1:6b). He'll finish that which He started in us.

OUR UNIQUENESS

As parents, we try to be sensitive to our children's uniqueness. Solomon said to *"train up a child in the way he should go: and when he is old, he will not depart from it"* (Prov. 22:6). Many of us stand on that Scripture when our backslidden children aren't going the way they've been reared. It's an awesome promise. However, there's much more depth to it. The word *"train"* (*chanak*) means "to initiate or discipline— dedicate, train up."[3] Though discipline can be to correct, it can also be a character trait we instill into our children that allows them to stay focused. The word *"initiate"* implies that they can also begin to foster those necessary traits to grow into the godly, responsible men or women they were made to be. *"In the way he should go"* has an implication of spiritual direction, but it also means to "do the training according to the unique personality, gifts, and aspirations of the child,"[4] and nurture or correct his natural tendencies. Is your child athletic or scientific? Does he like literature or music? Is he a mathematician or a writer? Is he extroverted or introverted? We parents spend our children's formative years looking for what will bring our budding flowers into full bloom. When our children have found a niche that fits, it will last until they're "old." See, just like our natural children, God brings His children along, too, in the way we should go based on our strengths, personalities, desires, and giftings. He made us, so He's aware that we're special, unique creatures that He crafted to fulfill our custom-made destiny.

Jeremiah 29:11 says, *"For I know the thoughts that I think toward you, saith the Lord, thoughts of peace, and not of evil, to give you an expected end."* What is that *"expected end"*? God knows, and we must trust He has our lives in His hands. We're called by Him for purposes that promote His Kingdom. As a separated people, we don't fit any mold: *"For ye see your calling, brethren, how that not many wise...mighty...*[or] *noble, are called"* (1 Cor. 1:26). Remember back in the Sheep Gate when we discovered God takes us through the gate just because He loves us? He chooses us, not because of our might, intelligence, education, or human strength, but because He'll get glory when He accomplishes His purpose through us, imperfect vessels. Many great leaders in past moves of God were inferior in the world's eyes—uneducated, antisocial, female, divorced. But on God's scales, they were just right. So are we.

Job says that, like the potter, God's *"hands have made me and fashioned me together round about..."* (Job 10:8). We are created vessels to do His work, in His time, in His way. We discovered in the Valley Gate that tribulations God has allowed during our journey have done an essential work, and sometimes we've even needed to go back to square one for Him to remake us *"again another vessel, as seemed good to* [him]*"* (Jer. 18:4). Those trips around the mountain, through the Valley and Dung Gates, or, as my dad would have said, "to the woodshed," played their roles in allowing us to reach our Assignment Gate. As the Potter works and reworks us, we become what *He* wants us to be, not what we desire. Romans 9:21 says, *"Hath not the potter power over the clay, of the same lump to make one vessel unto honour, and another unto dishonour?"* What we are is literally in the Potter's hands.

In the Fountain Gate, we learned how Holy Spirit gave gifts to help us get to the fullness of our ministry: prophecy, ministry, teaching, exhortation, giving, ruling, and showing mercy (see Rom. 12:6-8). No matter which job the Lord gives us, even if a million other people are assigned that same job, we're His own creation who do the task a special way, for none of us do our giftings alike but *"the same God which worketh all in all"* (1 Cor. 12:6b). First Corinthians 7:7 says these gifts are made in different manners, so though we all come through the same gates and learn similar lessons, we implement our gifts differently by God's design. We must discover and step into *Miphkad* as we fulfill the assignment God has crafted for us alone. Then, He uses that for His

Kingdom, and our *"gift maketh room for* [us], *and bringeth* [us] *before great men"* (Prov. 18:16). Wow, what a promise!

My daughters are identical twins. After they were born, their doctor told me I should try to foster their individualities. As a result, they rarely dressed alike. They wore different hairstyles. One primped relentlessly while the other was happy with a ponytail and no makeup. One was better at sports while the other excelled in academics. One was sassy; the other, subdued. Career choices were different; tastes in guys, cars, and clothes all varied. Even though their DNA is alike, they're unique. All of us who have the Lord's DNA are alike, yet different. We're wonderful, inimitable creations God has carefully crafted to fit into a place He made especially for us. Now that we're here, what could we ever hope to achieve that's better than a destiny custom-made by the Master's hands?

ANALOGIES FOR GROWTH

The Bible shows two perfect analogies to this journey of gates and its end here at *Miphkad*. If you check Appendices 2, 3, and 4, you'll see information for Ezekiel's river and the Wilderness Tabernacle. Ezekiel says four levels exist to growing deeper in God (see Ezek. 47:3-5). We get in up to our ankles as we learn about Him. Then we make a stronger commitment as we go into the river up to our knees. Those of us who want more, get deeper in Him by wading in up to our loins. Those who want all He has, eventually plunge in. The chart shows characteristics that go along with each phase. Like our walk through the gates, the river confirms that the stages that emerge into spiritual maturity are a progression. *Miphkad* is when we plunge in and no longer allow ourselves determine our own destiny but rather let the river, Holy Spirit, carry us wherever He wishes us to go.

The tabernacle is another analogy that connects to *Miphkad* (see Exod. 25–31). Three sections existed. As Appendices 3 and 4 show, we come first into the Outer Court where we begin to pay attention to God but still operate primarily in the flesh. If you'll refer one more time to Appendix 1, those gates on the west side of the city are Outer

Court experiences. They're the ones where, though we came into the Kingdom, we were still primarily focusing on "me" things—learning how God fits into *my* life, seeing things *I* must change, finding *my* foibles God wants to remove.

After the Fountain Gate, though, we're changed. That's when we enter the Holy Place where we still learn about God, but through the context of Holy Spirit, and focus more on *God* things rather than *me* things. We get the idea of being kings and priests, understand how Holy Spirit takes us into a deeper walk with Him, and know God is victorious. Then, *Miphkad* takes us into the Holy of Holies. That's where we learn to minister from the Mercy Seat and dwell in God's presence. We get there through worship at the East Gate, and that's where revelations of God's glory and manifestations exist. *Miphkad* is where Christians need ultimately to dwell and where God longs for us to be.

CONCLUSION

Several years ago, I began to feel dissatisfaction with my life. I pondered whether I should tell Wade about what was going on inside of me. Even though I thought he might feel I'd gone over the edge, one night before we went to sleep, I poured out my heart to him. I said I'd come to a place where I didn't care about anything as much as to be about the Father's business. I knew I still had a job to do, a house to keep, a husband to care for, children to rear. My heart, however, longed only for the time when I could minister for God.

After I spoke these words, Wade said nothing for a moment. I waited silently, wondering if he was thinking his wife had crossed over into fanaticism and was beyond what he'd signed up for. Finally, he just reached for my hand in the darkness. "Connie, I've felt that way myself for a long time and didn't want to say it to anyone, even you."

As he and I come into our own *Miphkad*, we look back at our lives' choices that have brought us to this place—his military experience, our careers, our child-rearing, our season of pastoring and evangelizing, our ministry growth. With each gate we came into, God said to us, "Connie, I still need to do some refining in you," or "Wade, if this doesn't get out of you, you can't withstand the fire," or, "Guys, I have a place for you, but you need to learn more of Me first." Each gate has brought us here, and wherever God takes us tomorrow, it's OK. The culmination of a walk He has chosen is better than any we may have planned for ourselves.

Twentieth-century American poet Robert Frost said in his poem "The Road Not Taken" that sometimes in life we have choices to make that will impact where we ultimately go:

"...Two roads diverged in a wood, and I—

I took the one less travelled by,

And that has made all the difference."[5]

There are lots of well-worn paths people take that may be easier, but the one where we make our own unique mark is the one that will make "all the difference," not just to us but also to those around us and to our posterity. We've now come full circle. Back in the Sheep Gate, we learned that Jesus made the same point in Matthew 7:13-14:

...wide is the gate, and broad is the way, that leadeth to destruction, and many there be which go in thereat: because strait is the gate, and narrow is the way, which leadeth unto life, and few there be that find it.

When we came to those roads that diverged and opted for the one that led to the Sheep Gate, we chose the one that was "less travelled." We started walking on it though we knew it had a *"strait...gate, and narrow...way,"* but we chose that and have continued on for this journey going further and deeper in Him. Along the way, many have dropped off because they yearned for the more populated, broader way. Now, here at *Miphkad,* numbers have become sparse and footprints few, but we're among those willing to pay that cost, those who came into the Sheep Gate, fell in love with the Shepherd, and continued on to this place, this time.

Oh, so long ago, the Potter threw a shapeless, noncompliant lump of clay onto His wheel. No one saw the potential He did, but He also knew the work that was ahead of Him. He ever-so-gently grasped that lump with His loving hands and began to shape it into what He had in mind. He worked, reworked, kneaded, and not-so-gently at times removed what couldn't remain. The process was laborious, and sometimes the end product seemed far away and even unreachable, but He continued, and the vessel ultimately complied. Finally, it was finished, shaped, fired, and painted, ready for whatever purpose the Potter had determined. Now, it's both beautiful and functional for each assignment where the Potter chooses to use His unique handiwork. This creation has learned throughout the journey what it was taught from the first and at every other gate since then. Just as a sheep learned to trust its fate to the hand of its Shepherd, the finished vessel learned that everything it has become is totally and utterly dependent on its Potter, the Father.

EPILOGUE

This book has been a progressive learning experience for both Connie and me. I have been amazed at how Holy Spirit continues to reveal more of Himself and our walk in Him at each of the gates. I am certain He will continue the revelation process in our lives, for He promises that *"ye shall seek Me, and find Me, when ye shall search for Me with all your heart"* (Jer. 29:13). This study of the gates demonstrates the progressive nature of our walk and the necessity of systematically entering each gate or phase of Christian experience as we grow in Christ. This process of discovery is shown throughout Scripture.

The Tabernacle in the Wilderness explains the process of entering into the Glory of God beginning with the Outer Court containing the Brazen Altar (a type of the Cross of Calvary) and the Bronze Laver (a type of washing of water by the Word). Then, an individual proceeded into the Holy Place containing the Golden Lampstand (a type of Holy Spirit), the Table of Showbread (a type of Lord Jesus Christ and the government of God), and the Golden Altar of Incense (a type of worship). Finally, the process culminated in the Holy of Holies with the Ark of the Covenant upon which the Glory of God resided. John described the spiritual maturation process of *"little children...young men...fathers"* (1 John 2:12-14). Paul, in his letter to the Romans, explains the progressive nature of freedom, beginning with being freed from wrath (see Rom. 5:9); from sin (see Rom. 6:11); from the law (see Rom. 7:6); and from the flesh. Now we're free to live in the Spirit (see Rom. 8:1-2). Our journey into conformity with

Christ is a *"little* [by] *little"* (Deut. 7:22), *"...precept upon precept...line upon line; here a little, and there a little"* progression (Isa. 28:10). The more we learn of God's ways and His progressive steps toward maturity, the fewer casualties we will have in the Body of Christ.

I believe we're in the beginning stages of a *kairos* time, a God-appointed time for a sweeping move of Holy Spirit throughout our land. God is preparing His people for this dynamic move of Holy Spirit through fresh revelation and new discoveries of the buried treasure of His truth. This study of the gates is one of these treasures we need to mine, bring to the surface, and process. As new converts come into the Kingdom, they can be introduced to the gates in a systematic progression that will lead them to maturity in Christ more effectively and efficiently. I have been blessed and spiritually equipped by having read this book, and I know you have as well.

I pray there will be a continued release in your life of...

...the spirit of wisdom and revelation...the eyes of your understanding being enlightened; that ye may know what is the hope of His calling, and what the riches of the glory of His inheritance in the saints, and what is the exceeding greatness of His power to us-ward who believe, according to the working of His mighty power, which He wrought in Christ, when He raised Him from the dead, and set Him...in the heavenly places, far above all principality, and power, and might, and dominion, and every name that is named, not only in this world, but also in that which is to come (Ephesians 1:17-21).

Amen.

—Wade Urban

APPENDIX 1

MAP OF JERUSALEM

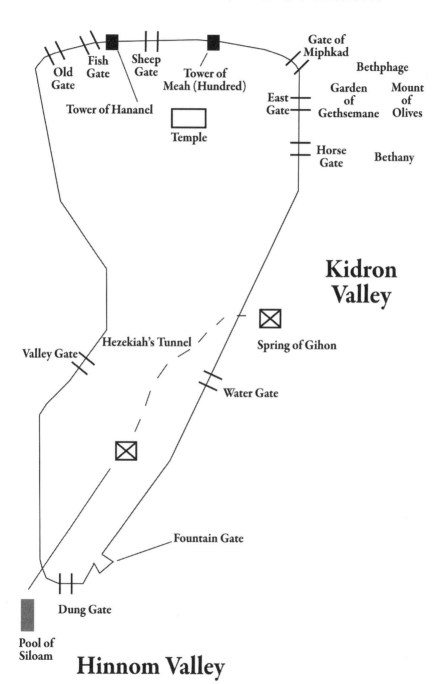

Gate of Miphkad

Bethphage

Fish Gate

Sheep Gate

Old Gate

Tower of Meah (Hundred)

Garden of Gethsemane

Mount of Olives

East Gate

Tower of Hananel

Temple

Horse Gate

Bethany

Kidron Valley

Hezekiah's Tunnel

Spring of Gihon

Valley Gate

Water Gate

Fountain Gate

Dung Gate

Pool of Siloam

Hinnom Valley

APPENDIX 2

LEVELS OF EZEKIEL'S RIVER

Ankle Deep	Knee Deep	Waist Deep	Waters to Swim in
You are:	You are:	You are:	You are:
...being refreshed.	...feeling the pull of Holy Spirit.	...experiencing fertility.	...learning to give yourself totally to the River.
...able to splash around.	...beginning to understand that there's more.	...assured that your reproductive parts are covered.	...in total submission.
	...trying harder to negotiate on your own.	...learning to flow in the Spirit.	...now part of Christ.
	...becoming more submissive to the River.	...able to make mistakes and recover.	...not able to get your own way because God is pulling you.
		...still thinking of it as "my ministry."	

APPENDIX 3

THE WILDERNESS TABERNACLE CHART

Outer Court	Holy Place	Holy of Holies
Inside:	*Inside:*	*Inside:*
Brazen altar (type of cross).	Golden lampstand (pure gold; represents Holy Spirit; illumination comes from this; represents revelation knowledge through gifts of Holy Spirit).	Ark of Covenant with the Glory of God residing on the Mercy Seat between the wings of the cherubim.
Bronze laver (washing of water by the Word; no dimensions for continual washing).		Ark was made of acacia wood overlaid with gold representing believers who are the temple of Holy Spirit (1 Cor. 3:16).
Items – wood overlaid (represents man being covered from judgment of God against sin).	Table of showbread (12 loaves = number of government; represents Jesus Christ; Isa. 9:6; also spiritual principle of dominion and representation with believers as kings and priests).	*Inside Ark:*
No covering—subject to natural senses.		Manna (represents provision and Word of God)
Represents hope.		Tablets of Moses (represents laws on our hearts)
	Golden altar of incense (lit from coal from brazen altar; smoke that comes from it is worship that permeates and fills the atmosphere with the fragrance of worship).	Aaron's rod that budded (represents resurrection life)
	Represents faith.	Represents love Himself.

APPENDIX 4

The Wilderness Tabernacle

HOLY OF HOLIES

MERCY SEAT
ARK

THE VEIL

|

GOLDEN ALTAR
OF INCENSE

HOLY PLACE

GOLDEN
LAMPSTAND

TABLE OF
SHOWBREAD

LAVER

THE OUTER COURT

BRAZEN
ALTAR

THE GATE

ENDNOTES

INTRODUCTION

1. "Interpreting Dictionary," *The Holy Bible,* King James Version (Gordonsville, TN: Dugan Publishers, Inc., 1984), 7.

2. Leland Ryken, James C. Wilhoit, and Tremper Longman III, eds., *Dictionary of Biblical Imagery* (Downers Grove, IL: InterVarsity Press, 1998), 923.

3. Ibid., 925.

4. Ibid., 321.

5. Ibid., 321-322.

CHAPTER 1

1. "Interpreting Dictionary," 3.

2. Ibid., 4.

3. Ryken, et. al., *Dictionary of Biblical Imagery*, 782.

4. Roberts Liardon, *God's Generals* (Laguna Hills, CA: Whitaker House, 1996), 263, 311, 408.

5. "Sheep," *The World Book Encyclopedia* (Chicago, IL: World Book, Inc. 1987), 306.

6. Ryken, et. al., *Dictionary of Biblical Imagery,* 784.

7. James Strong, LL.D., S.T.D., *King James New Strong's Exhaustive Concordance* (Nashville, TN: Thomas Nelson, Inc., 2001), #H7462.

8. Ryken, et. al., *Dictionary of Biblical Imagery*, 782.

9. Ibid.

10. Ibid.

11. Sarah Josepha Hale, "Mary Had a Little Lamb," *Once Upon a Time* (Chicago, IL: World Book, Inc., 2000), 50.

CHAPTER 2

1. Strong, *King James New Strong's Exhaustive Concordance,* #H5570.

2. B.A. Robinson, *Religious Tolerance.org.* 2009. Ontario Consultants on Religious Tolerance; http://www.religioustolerance. org/chr_symb.htm (accessed 24 April 2010).

3. Ibid.

4. Ibid.

5. "Christian Persecution." *UNRV History: Roman Empire.* 2003-2011. http://www.unrv.com/culture/christian-persecution.php (accessed 30 December 2011).

6. Ibid.

7. Ibid.

8. Ibid.

9. Ibid.

10. "Prophecy Fellowship." VBulletin Copyright. 2000-2010. Jellsoft Enterprises, Ltd.; http://www.prophecyfellowship.org/show thread.php?t=162186 (accessed 27 April 2010).

11. Ibid., "Comment."

12. Greg Long, "Fifteen"; http://www.lyricsvip.com/Greg-Long/Fifteen-Lyrics.html.

CHAPTER 3

1. Strong, *King James New Strong's Exhaustive Concordance,* #H3466, from #H3465.

2. "Interpreting Dictionary," 5.

3. Ibid., 8.

4. Ibid., 7.

5. Ibid., 2.

6. "Santayana, George." *Wikipedia: the Free Encyclopedia.* http://en.wikipedia.org/wiki/George_Santayana (accessed 27 April 2010).

7. Strong, *King James New Strong's Exhaustive Concordance,* #H5769.

8. Mark Twain, *Quotes Daddy.* 2008-2010 (accessed 18 August 2010). QuotesDaddy.com.

CHAPTER 4

1. "Interpreting Dictionary," 4, 10.

2. Ryken, et. al., *Dictionary of Biblical Imagery*, 909.

3. Ibid., 909-10.

4. "Joshua Chapter 10: The Miraculously Long Day." *Bible Study Manuals.* http://www.biblestudymanuals.net/joshua10.htm (accessed 3 February 2010).

5. Ryken, et. al., *Dictionary of Biblical Imagery*, 910.

6. Ibid., 910-11.

7. "Interpreting Dictionary," 1.

8. "Samson and Delilah." 20 March 2009. God: Apples of Gold in Pictures of Silver; http://www.picturesofsilver.com/Teachings/06judges5.htm (accessed 26 April 2010).

9. "Interpreting Dictionary," 9.

CHAPTER 5

1. "Interpreting Dictionary," 6, 8.

2. "Hinnom Valley." First Century Jerusalem; http://www.bible-history.com/eastons/G/Gehenna (accessed 27 April 2010).

3. Ryken, et. al., *Dictionary of Biblical*, 910.

4. "Birds," *The World Book Encyclopedia* (Chicago, IL: World Book, Inc., 1987), 250.

5. "Fish," *The World Book Encyclopedia* (Chicago, IL: World Book, Inc., 1987), 141.

6. "Insects," *The World Book Encyclopedia* (Chicago, IL: World Book, Inc., 1987), 216.

CHAPTER 6

1. Strong, *King James New Strong's Exhaustive Concordance*, #G4137 from 4134.

2. Jack Hayford, et. al., eds., *New Spirit Filled Life Bible* (Nashville, TN: Thomas Nelson Bibles, 2002), 1652, "Bottom Note."

3. "Interpreting Dictionary," 9, 3, 7.

4. Strong, *King James New Strong's Exhaustive Concordance*, #H4726.

5. Ibid., #H8210.

6. Ibid., #G1632, from #G1537.

7. Ibid., #G4215.

8. Ibid., #G4077.

9. "Meaning and etymology of the Hebrew name Gihon." Abarim Publications; http://www.abarim-publications.com/Meaning/Gihon.html (accessed 11 December 2011).

10. Hillel Geva. "Jerusalem-Water Systems of Biblical Times." 2010. American-Israeli Cooperative Enterprise. http://www.jewish virtuallibrary.org/jsource/Archaeology/jerwater.html.

11. Ibid.

12. Strong, *King James New Strong's Exhaustive Concordance*, #H2416 and #H4325.

13. Ryken, et. al., *Dictionary of Biblical Imagery*, 930.

14. Strong, *King James New Strong's Exhaustive Concordance*, #G1849.

15. Ibid., #G1411.

CHAPTER 7

1. "Merck Manuals: Introduction." *The Merck Manuals Online Medical Library*. 2009-2010. Merck and Co., Inc; http://www.merck. com/mmhe/sec12/ch158/ch158a.html (accessed 5 March 2010).

2. "Big Site of Amazing Facts." 2011. http://www.bigsiteof amazingfacts.com/why-does-your-body-need-water (accessed 30 December 2011).

3. Strong, *King James New Strong's Exhaustive Concordance*, #H4325.

4. Hayford, et. al., *New Spirit Filled Life Bible*, 923, Word Wealth."

5. "Interpreting Dictionary," 7.

6. Ibid.

7. Hayford, et. al., *New Spirit Filled Life Bible*, 1470, "Word Wealth."

8. Strong, *King James New Strong's Exhaustive Concordance*, #G2315.

9. Hayford, et. al., *New Spirit Filled Life Bible*, 1715, "Kingdom Dynamics."

10. Ryken, et. al., *Dictionary of Biblical Imagery*, 929.

11. Ibid., 930.

12. "Walking in Their Sandals: Jerusalem-Location Profile. 4 May 2010. http://www.ancientsandals.com/overviews/temple.htm.

13. *Susan W. Tanner, "Scriptures—More Precious Than Gold and Sweeter Than Honey," speech given 11 Sept. 2005, at Brigham Young University;* http://speeches.byu.edu/reader/reader.php?id=10576 (accessed *7 February 2010*).

14. "Ritual Purification." *Wikipedia: the Free Encyclopedia.* 24 February 2010. Wikipedia Foundation, Inc.; http://en.wikipedia.org/wiki/Ritual_purification (accessed 5 March 2010) and Ryken, et. al., *Dictionary of Biblical Imagery,* 931.

15. Ryken, et. al., *Dictionary of Biblical Imagery,* 931.

16. Hayford, et. al., *New Spirit Filled Life Bible,* 687,_ "Word Wealth."

17. Ibid., 279, "Center Reference."

18. Strong, *King James New Strong's Exhaustive Concordance,* #G739.

19. Kenneth L. Barker and John Kohlenberger III. *Zondervan NIV Bible Commentary*, Vol. 2. New Testament (Grand Rapids, MI: Zondervan Publishers, 1984), 915.

20. Strong, *King James New Strong's Exhaustive Concordance,* #G3875.

CHAPTER 8

1. "Interpreting Dictionary," 3.

2. Ryken, et. al., *Dictionary of Biblical Imagery,* 400-401.

3. Ibid., 400.

CHAPTER 9

1. Strong, *King James New Strong's Exhaustive Concordance,* #G2999.

2. Ibid., #G3050.

3. "Interpreting Dictionary," 9.

4. Ibid.

5. Bible History Online, "The Eastern Gate and Prophecy"; http://www.bible-history.com/gentile_court/TEMPLECOURTThe_Eastern_Gate_and_Prophecy.htm (accessed 6 May 2010).

6. Ibid., 6.

7. Ibid., 6, 8-10.

8. Ibid., 2-5, 8.

9. "Interpreting Dictionary," 5.

10. Strong, *King James New Strong's Exhaustive Concordance*, #G4352.

11. Ibid., 2, 5, 8.

CHAPTER 10

1. Strong, *King James New Strong's Exhaustive Concordance*, #H4662 and H4663.

2. "Interpreting Dictionary," 6-7.

3. Strong, *King James New Strong's Exhaustive Concordance*, #H2596.

4. Hayford, et. al., *New Spirit Filled Life Bible*, 829, "Bottom Note."

5. Robert Frost, "The Road Not Taken." 1920. Rpt. in Bartleby. com. 2011; http://www.bartleby.com/119/1.html (accessed 12 December 2011).

About
Connie Hunter-Urban

Married to Wade Urban, Connie was born in Oxford, Ohio, to Christian parents who pastored a Full Gospel church. She earned a B.A. degree in English and an M.A. degree in secondary education from Miami University in Oxford, Ohio. Connie taught high school English for 33 years, retiring in 2009. Connie and Wade have ministered as the Lord has led over the years. They have pastored, evangelized, taught, and mentored. They now publish a monthly newsletter, write books, speak at retreats and churches, conduct workshops, and minister fluently in the gifts of Holy Spirit with signs and wonders following. Connie's goal is to be about the Father's business.

You may contact Connie in the following ways:

Email: conniehunterurban@gmail.com
Address: P. O. Box 634
          Connersville, IN 47331
Phone: 765-825-2030
Website: restormin.org